The Turnaround Church

The Turnaround Church

Inspiration and Tools for Life-Sustaining Change

Mary Louise Gifford

THE
ALBAN
INSTITUTE
Herndon, Virginia
www.alban.org

The Alban Institute

2121 Cooperative Way, Suite 100

Herndon, VA 20171

Scripture quotations, unless otherwise noted, are from the New Revised Standard Version of the Bible, copyright © 1989, Division of Christian Education of the National Council of Churches of Christ in the United States of America, and are used by permission.

Scripture quotations noted as KJV are from The Holy Bible, King James Version.

Scripture quotations noted as NIV are from Holy Bible: New International Version, copyright ©1973, 1978, 1984. Used by permission of Zondervan Bible Publishers.

Cover design by Spark Design.

The artwork on page i is the logo of Wollaston Congregational Church (UCC) in Quincy, Massachusetts, whose story is told in these pages. It was created by Mary Arscott. The living tree at the center of the logo represents the congregation. Its lopsidedness is a reminder to allow room for growth. The open circle behind the tree symbolizes the congregation's openness to where God is leading, and the shadow in the form of a cross signifies that the congregation is steeped in Christian roots, connected to a deep and abiding faith.

Library of Congress Cataloging-in-Publication Data

Gifford, Mary Louise.

 The turnaround church : inspiration and tools for life-sustaining change / Mary Louise Gifford.

  p. cm.

Includes bibliographical references.

ISBN 978-1-56699-393-7

1. Church renewal. 2. Church growth. I. Title.

BV600.3.G54 2009

254'.5--dc22

2009032539

09   10   11   12   13   VP   5   4   3   2   1

Contents

.

Foreword

In the pages that follow, you will read a remarkable and inspiring story of the Wollaston Congregational Church, a formerly dying congregation that has, in only a few years, become once again a vibrant and exciting place of worship, hospitality, and service. At first glance, this account of an old "mainline" church that somehow managed to pull back from the brink of extinction and to achieve an abrupt turnaround may seem so rare and unexpected, so much an exception to the dismal rule of waning congregations, that it hardly seems useful to the rest of us. While it is uplifting, we may say, to hear how well it has gone for this one church, the Wollaston story can at first seem like a "hail Mary" pass, a miraculous, last-minute snatching of victory from the jaws of defeat, but not a game plan for any other congregation.

But this is where this book will surprise us. While the Wollaston story is not a recipe for other congregations to follow slavishly, it does show that congregational renewal is a realistic goal and that it comes, in part, through imaginative leadership, careful planning, community building, and attention to detail. As such, this book is an example of a new development in the literature of practical theology. Instead of studying pathology and trying to learn only from cases of failure, here we are invited to learn from healthy practices and strategies that have produced human flourishing.

Like a patient in intensive care, the Wollaston church had multiple systems collapsing all at once, and it needed strong intervention, quickly. One notable lesson of this book is to realize how the turnaround of this congregation happened not by a single "silver bullet" solution, but through energetic and comprehensive efforts on a variety of fronts: worship, stewardship, music, leadership, and institutional organization. The Wollaston church gained a fresh infusion of life not by desperately seizing some new and alien identity—a frenetic ecclesial extreme makeover—but by discovering and building upon the strengths already present in the community, by a thoughtful and creative renovation of the church's traditional patterns and structures.

At the center of this story stands an abundantly gifted and innovative pastor, Mary Louise Gifford. Gifford's training as a psychotherapist, combined with her experience as a community organizer, her contagious enthusiasm, her impressive interpersonal skills, and her indefatigable faith, has produced a pastoral leader of extraordinary vision and ability. When she answered the call to serve the Wollaston congregation, she was a freshly minted and unproven pastor and the church was in a steep and seemingly irreversible decline. But in that way of seeing that can only be attributed to the Spirit, each saw something of hope and promise in the other.

Several years ago, I had the privilege of being one of the leaders of a seminar for remarkable pastors, a group of carefully selected ministers and priests of outstanding achievement—in other words, a table full of church leaders like Mary Louise Gifford. Meeting periodically over a period of nearly two years, we read theology, analyzed cases, argued issues, and talked about pastoral leadership. One of the goals of the seminar, naturally, was to provide a fruitful season of continuing education for these pastors, but a second goal, frankly, was for me and the others on the leadership team to try to figure out what made these pastors tick, to discern what skills and ways of engaging ministry set them apart as superb practitioners of their pastoral art. The idea was that if we could identify how the best pastors do their work we could learn something about how to prepare and encourage others for creative and effective ministry.

At first, this second goal proved to be maddeningly elusive. Like Olympic skaters, these pastors performed at the very highest level, but they found it quite difficult to explain exactly how they glided through the pastoral figure eights, to analyze how they made decisions and did their ministry. Yes, they were well-trained and theologically knowledgeable. Yes, they had fine skills in counseling, preaching, teaching, organization, and leadership. Yes, they were dedicated to their work and to their congregations. But in any given situation of ministry, these skills, commitments, and areas of expertise were so fully integrated that they had become instinctive, a matter almost of "body knowledge." Thus, like high achievers in many fields, they were far better at doing than at describing. However, when encouraged—sometimes even pressured—to ever deeper levels of self-reflection, they were gradually able to name some of the individual threads and colors that composed the tapestry of their ministerial practice.

One of the gifts of this book is that Mary Louise Gifford has refined self-reflection to an art, and she can name the threads and colors of her ministry. She has the patience and insight to identify the parts that make up the whole of her notable leadership of the Wollaston congregation. We are able, for example, to watch Gifford weave a sound incarnational theology of money and possessions, a savvy psychotherapist's awareness of the power and danger of secrets in a family system, an ability to communicate in clear and effective ways, and a firm grasp of organizational principles into a revitalized stewardship emphasis for Wollaston.

But this book is far more than the narrative of Gifford's leadership, as outstanding as that has been. One of the most encouraging aspects of the Wollaston story is how clearly both Gifford and the congregation have felt the generous presence of God bringing streams of water to the desert places, giving new life and mission to a community of faith that had experienced defeat and despair. The turnaround at Wollaston Congregational Church is not merely an account of shrewd organizational management and institutional re-engineering. It is an Easter story, a story of God once again giving amazing and surprising new life, and the fact that Gifford tells it with such hopeful joy is evidence not only of her ability as a scribe but also of the depth of her faith.

Thomas G. Long
Author of *Beyond the Worship Wars: Building Vital and Faithful Worship*

Acknowledgments

This book is about the experiences of the members of the Wollaston Congregational Church United Church of Christ in Quincy, Massachusetts, in turning their church from a once-dying church to one that is filled with growth and vitality. There are many people I want to thank for helping me to write this book. Sarah Birmingham Drummond encouraged me to complete my doctoral dissertation, entitled "Fresh Eyes: The Living Experience of a Turnaround Church" in 2008, on which this book is based. My research professor, Elizabeth Nordbeck, pushed me to clearly define a turnaround church. Mark Heim, a member of my doctoral committee, captured the urgency of the work in a turnaround church when he commented about my work, "I have never read a dissertation that put theory into practice as fast as you did! You no sooner learned it than you applied it in your church."

The Calvin Institute of Christian Worship (CICW), funded by Lilly Endowment, granted our church funds in 2007 that allowed us to invite Thomas G. Long, the Bandy Professor of Preaching at Candler School of Theology at Emory University in Atlanta, Georgia, to spend a weekend at our church in Wollaston. Based on his book, *Beyond the Worship Wars: Building Vital and Faithful Worship*, our members were opened to a new understanding of the changes they could make to increase vitality in worship. Tom's inspiration continues to encourage us as our congregation evolves more fully into its call to health and vibrancy. My thanks go to Betty Grit, Worship Renewal Grants Program manager at CICW, for working with us so closely to make this happen.

Tom Clough, former associate conference minister of the Metropolitan Boston Association of the Massachusetts Conference of the United Church of Christ (MACUCC), supported me from the minute he told me our church would probably be the next in the conference to close and for all he did to help us to reverse that fate. My thanks also go to Wendy Vander Hart, our current area minister, who continues to nurture our denominational connection by encouraging our turnaround church. The MACUCC is a recipient of a Sustaining Pastoral Excellence grant from the Lilly Endowment, which funded a program where seasoned clergy mentor new members of the clergy. I was most fortunate to have been a part of this program for my first three years in ministry and during that time to be mentored by Judy Brain, a pastor of more than twenty years. Along with my colleagues John Hamilton, Karen Case, and Peggy O'Connor, who were also new ministers at that time, I benefited from Judy's many years of ministerial practice.

The staff of the Massachusetts Conference of the United Church of Christ has also supported me personally by sending Paul Nickerson to coach me in helping the church to grow from a dying church into our identity as a "new church start in our old church building." Paul's experience and talents helped me encourage the members of our congregation to find new life in the mission field outside their doors. Jim Griffith, founder of Griffith Coaching Network, has met with and coached the leaders of our congregation as we passed through stages from stabilization through turnaround to become the new church start we are today.

Editor Beth Gaede has been my rock throughout the process of writing this book. From our very first conversation in

Grand Rapids, Michigan, Beth has encouraged me to move forward in creating this book. I want to express my deep appreciation to the Alban Institute for providing me with such excellence in Beth, whose comments and suggestions have helped to make me a better writer.

I thank my spiritual director, Gini Wadsworth Pomeroy, who has walked beside me so patiently and listened for endless hours to my fears, hopes, and challenges in ministry. Ann Aaberg and Peter Johnston, colleagues and friends at Wollaston Congregational Church, have worked beside me, listening to my frustrations and longings to help this church be what I feel God is calling it to be.

My family has encouraged and supported me during what seems like a lifetime of weaving together academics and ministerial practice. My husband, Mark, has always been the guardian of the solitude I need to write. And my granddaughter, Fiona, inspires me more than I ever could have asked or imagined.

And finally, I want to thank the members of the Wollaston Congregational Church United Church of Christ for the opportunity to serve as their pastor for the past six years. Although only a few of you were there when I arrived in 2003, we have multiplied fourfold and welcomed thirty children into our church. And, my friends, we have only just begun!

Introduction

The mainline Protestant church is trying to recover from a deluge of cultural change over which it has not had control. The culture in which the mainline Protestant churches thrived in the 1950s has evolved in unpredictable ways over the last fifty-plus years. For example, many churches have experienced extreme decline in membership and shrinking financial resources, and many have disappeared from the landscape all across the country. The postmodern culture of today does not reflect the same Christian lifestyle of just two generations ago. And yet, people today are still asking the same question, "What is the purpose of my life?" a question the church has always tried to answer.

As the Pilgrims and the Puritans sought religious freedom in the new world in the sixteen hundreds, they grew a nation based on Christian values. In some parts of the New World, a town could not even be incorporated without a church. Membership in a church was critical for employment and was required for acceptance as a voting member of a town. Community life revolved around faith communities. The church provided a kind of moral and cultural fabric in the United States through the 1950s, when the church filled faith, community, and civic needs.

Since then the church has been affected by increasing individualism and self-reliance, geographic mobility, consumerism, distrust of clergy, and advanced technology. The way we define "family" is open to broader interpretation, and the effects of global politics have also fostered general resistance to religious institutions. Can the mainline Protestant church learn to adapt to the culture that surrounds it now and learn new ways to thrive again? And will the church be able to establish its relevance within this changed culture? To do so, the mainline Protestant church must reinvent itself. To carry the good news from generation to generation, members of congregations have to look at new ways of being the church within these new times. Churches were never meant to become static institutions, but rather to be living representations of Jesus Christ. Reinventing the church is a wonderful concept for the dying church, but how does one know where to start?

The beginning of the twenty-first century presents a unique opportunity for mainline churches to rediscover what we are and how to be relevant to a culture so drastically different from that of the 1950s, when this widespread decline began. Can we hold on to our Christian traditions and yet embrace the changes that will ensure the mission of Christ into the next century?

In this book, I will answer these questions by tracing the life of the members of the Wollaston Congregational Church United Church of Christ, through its decline in membership from more than nine hundred members in 1950 to its twenty-five worshipers in 2003. You will read about the decisions those twenty-five members made to call a new pastor, their first full-time pastor since the early 1980s, and the true story of how they became a turnaround church in this postmodern era, discovering a new mission right outside their doors.

I start with the premise that not all dying churches should die, and that under specific conditions, some can be brought back to a joyful life, filled with vitality. Through intentional changes in worship, stewardship, and leadership, some churches can and do succeed in turning around and beginning a new life, with renewed spiritual energy. As the pastor of this church, I know that it takes fresh eyes and deep abiding faith to lead people through the wilderness of change and into new ways of being a church.

Worshiping God in a community of believers is the reason we gather in the first place. Members of any church can begin the road to vitality by asking these questions: What is worship? How do we worship? Is our worship relevant to the community we serve today? Fueling the changes and enlivening the worship at Wollaston have been preaching, children, music, and art.

Questions regarding stewardship led the way for significant change in our congregation as well. I asked myself many questions: Can anyone get an overall snapshot of the financial picture of the church? How is the church's money collected and dispersed? Are the finances transparent? Is the pastor privy to members' pledge amounts? What resources are available outside the church? You will read that professional consultants paved the way to help us to change these practices as I discuss the day-to-day care and distribution of money in our church.

We also asked questions about leadership. How does one assume a position of leadership within this church? Are the church's bylaws of term limits for officers observed? What qualifications are needed for a member to hold a position of leadership? What role does the denomination play here? Methods from business and education have helped shape new practices in leadership in our church.

As the turnaround pastor of the Wollaston Congregational Church United Church of Christ, I was called to serve this dying church. The members of the search committee told me that they wanted to grow and change. Four and one-half years into our turnaround, I interviewed ten members who were active in 2003 and had remained so in those later years. I wanted to understand what this process of change had been like for them. I wanted to capture their experience. Some of their responses are highlighted in boxes throughout the book.

My goal in writing this book is to inspire leaders, lay and clergy, in other congregations to consider the potential for their church to turn around. In chapter 1, I will explore some factors that have contributed to the decline of the mainline Protestant church in the past fifty years. In the next three chapters, I will describe the methods that helped the people of the Wollaston Congregational Church United Church of Christ reverse the trend of dying churches in theirs. Through changes in worship, stewardship, and leadership practices, the topic of each of these three chapters, members have been ushered into a new identity and a new life in Christ. Our experience can provide examples for others who have the faith and courage to step into the hard work of reinventing the church for the people of tomorrow. Cultural influences aside, a turnaround church will bring fresh luster to tired eyes as the people of God live into new and exciting ways of being a vital and relevant church today.

Lewis Carroll is quoted as saying, "If you don't know where you're going, any road will get you there." Our church needed to decide where it was going and then how it was going to get there. In the final chapter, I will describe the vision and mission of the church, and tell you about some unexpected surprises along the way.

Throughout the book, I will be offering various tools that helped us turn our church around that you might consider using in your own church. One example is how to make deeper connections with your local conference and wider denomination and to learn about the resources they can offer to you. This book includes many examples of how we became a more hospitable congregation and how that hospitality is helping to grow our church. Ultimately, our attention to worship, stewardship, and leadership is bringing us into the mission work that calls us to grow deeper in Christ.

Although I have faced the many challenges at Wollaston with optimism and a brave heart, at times over these years I have been brought to my own knees before God, praying—and sometimes even begging—for guidance. Turning a church around can be a long and arduous process. We had to believe that God had not left us alone. Unaided by us, and deep into the dark of night, God's own Holy Spirit returned to this place, shedding new light all around and within us. That same Spirit has whispered new life into the heart and soul of our church, proving once again that resurrection still happens!

Chapter 1

The Turnaround Church

Then he said to me, "Prophesy to these bones and say to them, 'Dry bones, hear the word of the LORD! This is what the Sovereign LORD says to these bones: I will make breath enter you, and you will come to life. I will attach tendons to you and make flesh come upon you and cover you with skin; I will put breath in you, and you will come to life. Then you will know that I am the LORD."
—EZEKIEL 37:4-6, NIV

The *turnaround* church I am writing about was once thriving in ministry, membership, mission, music, and money. Due to a variety of factors over an extended period, the church had experienced such dramatic decline in these areas that it was considering closing its doors. To be a turnaround church, all of these conditions had to be reversed and new energy felt in the congregation. The church had been in decline not by reason of a sudden change in leadership or other more immediate variables. This slow decline took place over thirty-five to fifty years.

Wollaston Congregational Church
United Church of Christ

The Wollaston Congregational Church United Church of Christ, a church that in 2003 fit all of the criteria for a dying church, has found new life and purpose in its turnaround. The church is tucked on beautiful Wollaston Hill, in the northwest corner of the historic city of Quincy, Massachusetts, only twenty minutes south of Boston. In the 1950s, this church had more than nine hundred members. When I arrived as the new pastor of the church in 2003, the very large stone building was in terrible condition, and the people who actively participated in the life of the church numbered barely twenty-five. They only had enough money to stay open for three more years. Fifty years of decline was evident in both the small number of remaining people and in the decaying building. The air was filled with desperation.

As a newly ordained minister, I entered into a covenantal relationship with God and the congregation of Wollaston church as their pastor. I had just celebrated my fifty-third birthday. My professional background as both a psychotherapist and a community organizer had taught me to see beyond what was evident, to look deeper, and to find something positive, the hidden gems in this church. On my first tour of the facility, I was shown a stage in the parish hall. As strange as that might sound, that stage was the positive thing I knew I could build upon. I knew it would take time, but in my mind I could see some of the lively performances that might have taken place in the past and imagine those that might take place in the future. Sometimes imagination is all it takes for someone with a vision, like me, to see with fresh eyes of possibility. In fact, my mother once said that I would die of terminal optimism.

That optimism was contagious in the congregation. The church was incorporated in 1876 and celebrated its 130th anniversary in May 2006. This later date is particularly significant because when I began my ministry there in 2003, the treasury had only enough money for the church to stay open another three years. The anniversary was also noteworthy because not only was the church still open to celebrate the anniversary, but its members also felt hopeful about the future.

Today, many churches from different denominations are facing very serious decline in the same areas as our Wollaston church had. Decreasing numbers in worship, smaller numbers of volunteers to do the work of the church, and old buildings in need of costly repairs are the situations prompting many congregations to ask questions about their future. Some churches have members who no longer even live near the church and have lost touch with their neighbors surrounding their church. Quiet conversations are taking place everywhere about the relevance of the church in its neighborhood and whether even to try to reach out to the new neighbors. Options for these churches include, but are not limited to, turnarounds, merging or yoking with another church, adoption by larger churches, or closing down and using the existing buildings as sites for new church starts. Another option is to sell the buildings and use the money to help other churches continue their ministry. These were some of the decisions the folks at Wollaston had to wrestle with as we moved forward into an uncertain future of our own. When we began our work together, we had never even heard the term *turnaround church*.

The first three years of hard work paved the way for that 130th anniversary celebration and for a hopeful vision for our church, which, as I now write, has brought us six years into that future. We felt the presence of the Holy Spirit and sensed God's call to become something new. With God's help, our church has been resurrected. We learned that even in the worst-case scenario, as you will read about in the next few paragraphs, God is present. Proverbs 16:3 guided us: "Commit your work to the LORD, and your plans will be established."

When I accepted the call to serve God at the Wollaston church, little did I know that the church would soon be described to me in a way that caused my stomach to do a flip-flop. I was invited to have lunch with Thomas Clough. At that time, he was the area minister of the Metropolitan Boston Association of the Massachusetts Conference of the United Church of Christ. Tom was charged with oversight and support to the eighty-seven churches and their pastors in the association, although when we began talking, I didn't know the exact number. So when he said to me, "The Wollaston Congregational Church United Church of Christ is number eighty-seven," I naively asked, "Eighty-seven out of how many?" "Out of eighty-seven," he said. Then, I asked, "Are you saying it is the *bottom of the barrel*?" "Um-hum," he replied.

I will never forget that conversation. I could have walked away right then and there. But, being a person who loves a challenge and who is blessed, as I said, with terminal optimism, I decided to stay and to give it my all. In hindsight, I understand that not every declining or dying church is meant to live. Not all churches can or should turn around. But there are some, like Wollaston, that have a will to live and at least a strong sense of God's call to try. Six years later, our work together has defined us as "a new church start in an old church building." Our story can lend hope to others in similar circumstances. Telling you what we actually did to change will offer some fresh ideas that could inspire a similar transformation in your own church.

The situation at Wollaston was urgent. With so little money in the bank and so few people in the pews, the members were willing to take the risk to hire a full-time minister. I was a brand new seminary graduate, a risk that many established congregations are not willing to take. The members were willing to listen to me and to one another and to risk it all together. So was I. We seemed to be a match made in heaven, or as the apostle Paul might have aptly called us, we were fools for Christ.

My immediate predecessor was an interim minister who had served for the eighteen months before my arrival. Shortly before I was called, he had already agreed to serve another church in the same community. At Wollaston, he had followed a minister who had served the church part time for seventeen years. That pastor had not been called to be the settled, or long-term, pastor until he had already served for ten of those years.

I cannot say that I had a concrete plan in place when I began my work with the congregation. I wish I could give clear-cut directions and outline a process that I had in hand when I began. But I cannot. Looking back, I can only say that I had to begin at the beginning. But how did I know what to do? I had to ask myself, what had this congregation asked me to do, and what was God calling me to do?

Members of the congregation desperately wanted their church to survive and thrive into the future. They wanted to grow in members. They wanted children to come. They wanted to build a financial future for the church with new leadership to take them to these new heights. They knew

they needed to repair their building. I believed that God had
called me to help them. To get from here to there, I needed
to examine their practices of worship and their outreach to
the community, their practices of hospitality, and what programs they offered for children. I also needed to understand
their stewardship practices and get a sense of their leadership. As you read further, you will understand why I thought
the congregation needed to address these particular areas
and that they had to be looked at simultaneously.

Worship and Hospitality

Drawing on my own experience as a parent and as an adult
visiting this church for the first time, I looked around and
asked myself what would have prevented me from coming
to this church or bringing my own children here when they
were young. I tried to see both what was apparent and also
what was missing for me. As a parent, I learned that the congregation did not have an organized Sunday school program.
I noticed that several older youth who, although they attended the beginning of the worship service, left to go somewhere
else in the building for what they called Sunday school. But
it turned out that they had no adult supervision, no curriculum was in place, and they were pretty much on their own
to just talk with one another. There were several younger
children with whom the older teens tried to interact, but
without adult guidance and supervision, this fizzled quickly.
I had learned about "Safe Church Policies and Procedures"
for Sunday school, which requires having at least two adults
present in every Sunday school classroom.[1] I did not have
much experience with how to organize a Sunday school, so
I looked back at the church that had been my home church
for the fifteen years before I attended seminary. The model

they used for Sunday school was that it met at the same time as the worship service. Children from different classes came into the sanctuary with their teachers several times a year to hear a children's message from one of the pastors. But at Wollaston, the people told me they wanted the children to begin every worship service with the congregation and then to go to Sunday school as the service progressed. The practices at Wollaston were already at odds with my training and with my expectations as a parent.

The three large classrooms in the Christian education wing were in need of an update. The walls were painted with strong, bold colors, out of sync with my understanding of the more subdued colors appropriate for a learning environment. The space felt neither hospitable for children nor conducive to learning. I thought these two barriers—a disorganized Sunday school and unsuitable space to learn—would be glaring concerns for new families bringing their children to the church and to Sunday school.

Next, I tried to put myself into the shoes of an adult visiting for the first time. I asked myself how I was greeted and welcomed into the congregation. First, the building had no signs in or on it to tell me where I was in this very large space. I asked myself, what were the habits of the people, as few as they were, in welcoming new people? Were they really the friendly church they claimed to be? How had they welcomed me, a stranger, into their fold? My home church, a congregation of six hundred members, was again my reference point, where pastor, greeters, and deacons welcome each person, new and old, coming into the building for worship. Upon my arrival at Wollaston, I thought the remaining twenty-five active members might perhaps invite me to their homes for dinner or even a cup of tea. But, in my first year at the church, only two members invited me to their homes at all.

Several members told me right out that because of my organizational skills and sense of order, they would never invite
me to their homes, because they thought my standards were
too high. Although I felt disheartened, I fortunately realized
that said a lot more about them than it did about me.

I also got the impression that some members considered
the church an extension of their homes and, in fact, treated
the church like their own personal clubhouse, feeling free to
leave their belongings wherever they liked and for as long as
they liked. Church closets were brimming with their personal belongings. I was quite surprised that even the church records and valuable archival materials were sitting in piles on
shelves in the office supply room. Policies about who could
use the building and space were fuzzy at best, and there didn't
seem to be the order I was used to in my home church. Who
was responsible for what, I wondered? A lack of boundaries
around space was a problem.

Hospitality in general, the Sunday school, and boundary
and space issues were areas for me to focus on right away. I
had come in with the false assumption that in a church more
than a hundred years old, an organized and well-run Sunday
school and hospitality in worship were givens. With these issues identified, I could now begin to work on change. I, like
Dorothy in *The Wizard of Oz*, knew I was "not in Kansas any-
more!" But, where was I?

They had called me to help them change, but what kinds
of changes would they tolerate, I wondered. In the next chapter, you will read the story of the changes we undertook to
grow our Sunday school and to include children in worship
each week, and how we are living into the hospitality model
of our denomination, which states, "No matter who you are
or where you are on life's journey, you are welcome here."[2]
But first, I want to give you more of my first impressions.

Stewards of Buildings and Finance

The stewardship of the deteriorating building and the financial life of the church were the next two areas I turned to. There are two buildings, a parish house built in 1915 and the sanctuary built in 1925, connected as one large building by indoor hallways. The care and upkeep of the buildings had been neglected after suffering years of continuous water damage. Due to ever-dwindling funds for maintenance and repairs, it seemed that over the past two decades, money and attention had only been allocated for quick fixes and not to long-term solutions. I asked myself, how could we raise the money to preserve this architectural gem? Many New England church buildings are one or two hundred years old, and some even older. They are very costly to maintain, and the cost of heating them can be out of sight. These buildings, beautifully crafted to accommodate hundreds of people in worship, can drain money and energy from the current congregations.

The members of the Wollaston congregation told me they wanted to improve the church's financial situation. Given that they had only enough money to stay open for three more years, they wanted me to help them change that forecast quickly, but it took me a while to get at the roots of their financial despair. I noticed that when discussing a situation, their conversation always began with, "Well, the problem is . . ." and I never heard a word about a solution. They had not had the wherewithal to add to the church treasury for decades, and this had contributed to a full-blown financial crisis. The squeeze they felt was very real, and they would need some education in how to operate as a small nonprofit. Churches need money to operate. Yes, time and talent are necessary, but conversations about the buildings and the money had been neglected and were long overdue at Wollaston. It is a well-known fact that people would rather share the most intimate details of their lives with others, but don't ask them about their money! This was true in our church. In chapter 3, you will read about how we are addressing the finances and the repairs of the building. We want to ensure the usage of the building for at least another century and build up the treasury for future generations of the church. These are our responsibilities.

Leaders in the Church

One of my concerns was the feeling of negativity among the church leaders, which led me to feel uneasy with the leadership. The small group of members had only been looking to each other for answers. They were tired. Their constant struggle to keep the church open had zapped their energy, so coming up with creative solutions to some of the problems they were facing on their own was difficult for them. They were exhausted. The biggest collisions eventually occurred among the church's leaders. In fact, almost half of them left the church within my first year as pastor.

When I looked at the leadership of the church, I asked myself, how does a church unstick itself from the past while continuing to respect its Christian roots and traditions? And simultaneously, how does it open itself to new and creative ways of being a church together? I wondered how the Wollaston church had remained separate from rapid changes in business operations that newer technology offered. How did it reflect global economics that have changed the worldview of many Americans? Churches are not immune to the culture around them, and yet some kind of invisible insulation had kept this church from developing practices that reflected the changes all around it. As churches, we are called to address the changing culture and to respond to the needs of a dynamic and ever-changing people. How could I even begin this conversation while such a strong loyalty to the past kept my congregation isolated from these changes?

Of course, in retrospect, this is clearer, but back in 2003, I wondered how certain people had risen to the roles of leaders in this church. Here is an example to illustrate. Within my first month as pastor, some of the leaders had organized a three-day event that gave me a clue to just how glued to the past they really were. This event centered on the church of old as depicted in the book *At Home in Mitford*, the first book in a series by Jan Karon called The Mitford Years.[3] The story follows the life of one middle-aged bachelor minister as he falls in love with the woman next door. They lived out their lives in this tiny, fictional town of yesterday called Mitford. The Mitford event, which included members dressed as characters from the book, an outdoor concert, and special photographs of "Father Tim" (the main character) and his dog, was well attended and did bring the community together, but for what purpose? I wasn't sure, but the pining among the members for the small-town feeling of yesterday was palpable. The congregation really seemed to appreciate the enormous effort that went into organizing this entire event. It was curious to me that these same few people seemed to have done all of the organizing and planning for the church for many years.

The members were tired of struggling for so long that they were happy when anyone had an idea, and they let them run with it. They felt that doing something was better than doing nothing. I got a sense of a people who were going around in circles without a direction. I wondered whether concerns about power and control were lying beneath the surface. I

VISION

also wondered, what was the role of the pastor in this church? What did they expect from me? I will say a lot more about the church's leadership in chapter 4, but it seemed that many had lost sight of their church's purpose; like sheep, they seemed to have lost their way. The Bible tells us that without vision, the people perish (Prov. 29:18 KJV). What was their vision?

My heart ached with compassion for the members of Wollaston, and I began to fall in love with them right from the start. I had been called to discover and to change some of the patterns and practices that were killing their church. I likened their church to a boat. They had called me to sail the boat by granting me the authority to lead them. They wanted me to bail the boat because it was literally taking on water. They wanted me to steer the boat and lead them in a new direction. But they also wanted me to rock the boat, because some of those in the boat had to be shaken up and out. And they wanted me to help them build a new boat in which they all felt spiritually fed and empowered to do the mission and ministry of the church. Simultaneously, they wanted me to keep their boat afloat by staying true to the traditional Christian roots of the faith. Could I deliver all that? Could anyone?

Worship, Stewardship, and Leadership

So, this is how worship, stewardship, and leadership became my focus. These seemed to be the aspects of congregational life that cried out for change. To break it down even further, in worship, we focused on hospitality, children in worship, and building a Sunday school. At the same time, we addressed areas of stewardship of the buildings and property, as well as the finances. It became clear that I had to lead first by example and then by developing leaders. This is how I developed a type of road map to follow and, ultimately, led the congregation into significant changes that would transform them into a turnaround church.

With my road map in hand, I knew that I would have to combine all my skills with those of the congregants and be very creative in approaching these congregational changes. Relying on God's Spirit in each of us, I had to jar the stagnant energy and negative patterns in the church. I had to help the members get themselves unstuck from each other and from the past. The members had given me a real gift, in that they had called me to help them change. Not all pastors are given such clear permission to lead their congregations in ways that will change the church's direction. Due to the situation's urgency and magnitude, my congregation vested me with pastoral authority right from the start. What skills would I need to lead the congregation into and through the changes they so desperately wanted and needed?

My Personal and Professional Background

I brought both personal and professional experiences with me to Wollaston, and I believed that my skills matched the congregation's needs. I knew I had some skills to lead the way. Early in my seminary experience, I enrolled in a systematic theology course. The first assignment was to write a one-page paper answering the question, "Where do you draw authority from?" I think the professor was expecting answers that included the Bible and various well-known religious thinkers over the ages. I, however, had not even completely read the Bible when I entered seminary. I thought they would teach it to me there. I viewed my own spiritual experience and authority from a different perspective. In the paper, I claimed my authorities in authors and leaders in the self-help movement of the 1980s—Caroline Myss, Claudia

Black, Hannah Hurnard, Sharon Wegscheider-Cruse.[4] To me, they also walk on holy ground. As a card-carrying member of that self-help movement, I used them as my experts, along with every 12-step and self-help book and organization I had found in my own personal journey. Their books had led me through serious personal change. Authority, as I had come to understand it, after rejecting the notions of the religious authority I had experienced in the Catholic Church of my childhood, came from my own personal experience with God. These experts I have mentioned gave me the freedom to discover my own understanding of God, permission they had offered to me in their books. I admit my perspective was and continues to be that of one schooled in life, my own life, and not steeped in literature of the past. The flexibility of my own thinking about various spiritual disciplines and my own personal transformation proved to be a blessing to the congregation at Wollaston, for I was spiritually nimble.

Throughout the 1980s, when I was in my thirties, I had a number of spiritual awakenings. You might remember that was when the self-help movement emerged and swept across America. In addition to the authors I named above, John Bradshaw and Rokelle Lerner, authors and lecturers, equipped the twenty-seven million Adult Children of Alcoholics in this country with spiritual and educational information that offered many new choices.[5] These authors introduced me to terms like *dysfunctional family, family of origin,* and *family of affiliation* to provide a framework to help me, and many people like me, let go of past hurts of living with an alcoholic parent and to conceive of a future with hope, health, and happiness. Reading Bradshaw and Lerner further reinforced for me the hope and inspiration offered by Black and Wegscheider-Cruse. This combination of authors, lecturers, and 12-step programs helped me understand myself as well as my family of origin by educating me and introducing me to new possibilities for understanding God. I referred to their work with dysfunctional families and applied it to the church in Wollaston, a dysfunctional system or a dysfunctional church. I found these terms helpful in understanding a broken system and did not use them to make judgments about the church or the people.

A concept I found particularly helpful was denial, a psychological defense mechanism that becomes highly developed in those living in dysfunctional systems. In order to cope with situations far beyond their control, children and adults often develop a kind of fantasy world in which they can tell themselves, "My situation is not that bad," when in fact, it is very bad. At Wollaston, members' denial helped preserve what they had had and kept them distanced from the pain of the reality of their dying church. Denial serves to protect people from their own helplessness. Denial helps people or institutions preserve what they once had for a future time when they might have more control of their circumstances. The move from denial to reality can come at any time, but usually it is not accomplished without intervention of some kind. Because denial involves a type of blindness to reality, intervention is necessary to help people see their circumstances more clearly. One of the reasons church turnaround experts believe that it takes a new pastor to lead a congregation through a turnaround is because the old pastor becomes enmeshed into the system of denial along with the congregation. The exception is when a particular experience or set of circumstances causes a transformation in the settled pastor's heart.

Having myself grown up in a dysfunctional family and overcome my own denial, I almost immediately recognized the patterns of denial in the congregation. Just as each of the authorities I mentioned above had coaxed me out of denial back in the 1980s, I needed to coax some of the people at Wollaston out of their denial about their church and empower them through education to make new choices. The congregation at Wollaston needed intervention, the kind I knew of, to help members focus on the present rather than the past. Although they had functioned as a church for many years by following the church bylaws and living up to their commitments on boards and committees, their church was still dying. I needed to help them to remove their own blinders about worship, stewardship, and leadership to help them to see and be able to say aloud, "Yes, it is that bad," and to ask themselves and each other, "What can we do differently?" Although these sentences are short, the journey of transformation was not. Fortunately, my call to help this congregation change meant that they had given me permission to tell them the truth as I saw it.

Turning a church around involves a number of years dedicated to dismantling old systems and initiating and implementing newer, more effective systems. This is one of the major obstacles that points out the difference between a new church plant and a turnaround church. Although a new church plant does have its own set of challenges, it does not carry the same baggage as a turnaround church. At Wollaston, that baggage sometimes seemed overwhelming. As I walked around the church buildings, I saw physical plant issues everywhere. I saw holes in the walls, paint peeling, walls caving in, closets stuffed with papers and other remnants of the past. Water came into the building every time it rained. Members of the congregation had learned to close their eyes to all of this decay, a form of visual denial. The building smelled of mildew all summer, and they couldn't even use the copy machine in the summer because of the dampness in the office. Wouldn't you have done something about this? The work seemed overwhelming and eventually they just ignored it. The members had become accustomed to making broken things work as long as possible. They had not put serious effort into repair of the church building. It seemed as if they had simply lost heart because of the odds, and their collective denial allowed them to feel okay and that they and their church were safe. Yet, they also felt trapped in a situation for which they could not find any solutions, so they knew that they would not be able to sustain their church because their building and finances were about to give out. I think they felt powerless, but still they had not given up hope. That was when they called me as their first full-time pastor in decades, their first female pastor ever, and they asked me to help them change. I wondered if their previous pastoral leaders, the ones they had trusted to take them to the promised land, had disappointed them. I wondered why the church had not kept up with the culture surrounding it, which had changed so much.

When I surveyed the scene with my fresh eyes, I could almost see a cloud of negativity that had hovered over the congregation and had dampened members' creativity. Remember my terminal optimism? Well, even under that cloud, I could feel my own excitement, enthusiasm, and creativity bubbling. I couldn't wait to get started. That energy would eventually become contagious. Change, however, is almost always accompanied by some kind of crisis. I believed that my life skills had also given me the patience to watch carefully for whatever crisis would erupt at Wollaston. People do not necessarily resist change, but rather they resist loss. And much was at stake to lose.

In accepting the call to Wollaston, I believed that God had a calling not just for me but also for the congregation. My job, as I came to understand it, was to use all of my experience, gifts, and skills—personally, professionally, and prophetically—to help the people grow a new church within their old church and in the process help them grow a new heart for God and for the mission of their church. It is a paradox, I know, but to turn this church around from old to new, I knew that the people might have to feel worse before they began to feel better. And they did. None of what I am going to tell you in the next chapters has been easy, but we know that God has been with us every step of the way, from the congregation's decision to call me as their pastor and invest authority in me, to their collective hope of a future for their church.

Turnaround churches are a rare phenomenon in the mainline Protestant denominations of the United States. Our church became the first turnaround church to be recognized by the Massachusetts Conference of the United Church of Christ. We were able to change the course of our own history by interrupting the course of fifty years of decline. By exposing the denial and by opening ourselves to the truth of possibility about the church, most, but not all, of those who lived under the cloud of denial again sing God's praises. Not everyone made it, but those who stayed have found reasons to rejoice in God's finding favor in their church.

As I write this story in 2009, with seventy-five to eighty regular Sunday worshipers, thirty children enrolled in the Sunday school, and new faces in worship almost every week, you can see that we have come a long way. In the next three chapters, I will focus on the changes in worship, stewardship, and leadership that have transformed our congregation and our church.

Chapter 2

Worship

Once upon a time church bells rang out to summon the whole village, but we no longer live in that village. We live instead in a fragmented, diverse society in which a cacophony of bells clangs for our attention.
—THOMAS G. LONG, *BEYOND THE WORSHIP WARS*

When I told a woman who had grown up in our community that I was serving at Wollaston Congregational Church, she told me she thought it had been closed for years. That is how dead the church had appeared for a long time to the outside world. As I look back on the first few times I worshiped with my new congregation, my first impressions were consistent with that outsider's perspective. First, the cavernous sanctuary, which is built to seat six hundred people, seemed massive for the twenty-five people in worship in 2003. Second, the people sat scattered throughout the pews and not with each other. Third, a few people seemed to stand out during the announcement time, almost as if no one else had anything to say. The congregation felt lost and disconnected to me. The space had no energy. It felt breathless.

Although the order of worship followed a traditional pattern for a Protestant worship service, the environment seemed to lack the luster I was accustomed to elsewhere. My senses had been honed over many years of studying the anatomy of energy through such experts as author and lecturer Caroline Myss.[1] I tried to feel my way to understand what was missing. Had the Spirit left this church, I wondered. How does one breathe life back into a breathless tomb? Hmmm. Jesus came to mind.

I needed to look at the situation through fresh eyes. I had to envision what was not there and begin to see this congregation not as it was but as the church it would become. Yes, worship felt breathless, but not dead. Where was God's Spirit hiding? Where were the children? Where was the art? Why was the music so lifeless? And why didn't the people sit with one another? I had so many questions as I began to fill in those empty spaces with visions of the future.

In my mind, I went back to my call. Remember, the congregation wanted me to rock the boat because they wanted to change. My call was to sail the boat, because they needed to keep moving; to steer the boat, because they wanted a new direction; to bail the boat, because it was leaking and we had to keep it until we could build a new boat that would sustain the congregation into the future. Where should I begin?

I decided to start with worship, because is it the primary purpose for our Sunday morning gatherings. But we would not have a building to worship in if I didn't also start with stewardship. And I needed to immediately show the people a model of inspirational and creative leadership. The process of change would involve all three, worship, stewardship, and leadership simultaneously. I was ready. I imagined I had a spiritual army behind me, and Jesus in front of me as I stepped up to their expectations and the challenges we faced.

Perhaps that is when the Holy Spirit became reenergized in this church.

So, where were the children? And where would I find leaders to help with worship? And if music can be up to 50 percent of the worship service, how would I go about enlivening the music? I interviewed ten members of the church four and one-half years into our turnaround, and in these next sections, first I will give the question, then give several of the people's responses, and then tell you in detail what we did to make the changes they are responding to.

Children in Worship

How has having the children in worship each week has affected you? Can you give a specific example of a time when you benefited from a children's message?

- I don't know how much the kids get out of it, but the adults love it.
- I love to hear the children praying in worship.
- I used to give the children's message a lot. I liked to talk about the Civil War.
- I like the way we are teaching the children about the mission work of the church and explaining what will be done with the money we collect here for the community and connecting them to the wider world.

I quickly saw that the church offered nothing that would attract parents and children. The building could support a very large Sunday school program, which it had in years past. Some of the members had tried to organize a vacation Bible school the summer before I came, but when no children showed up, they decided simply to go through the class themselves, which seemed odd to me. Why would adults use a children's curriculum? I think it would have made sense for them to rethink how they had advertised the program for children and develop another strategy. The fact that they did not do this helped me realize that the organizers would benefit from training in leadership.

First, however, I had to learn more about the dynamics of the small group of people who were organizing events in the church. Could I help them see that their methods did not produce the growth or development they longed for? What kind of leadership had brought them to this place? I saw them as a tightly knit circle of people holding hands for dear life. They had no room between them for new people or new ideas. In chapter 1 I described our church as a dysfunctional system. One of those dysfunctions is called codependency, unhealthy patterns of dependence that stunt growth in individuals. I had to get them unstuck from one other and create some breathing space between them to see if I could discover some independent thoughts. When I spoke with most of the people individually, they responded by telling me not what they thought, but rather what someone else thought. This is another sign of codependence. Each time I asked one particular person a question, she answered with another person's opinion or a long story from the past. Getting some folks to talk about the present was difficult, and I got the clear sense that many were living in another era.

From my background in psychology, I knew that to change, a person has needs to have at least 60 percent of his or her mental energy in the present. Many of these folks lived in the past, and many of their reference points were those of their parents and their parents' peers. I wondered how it happened that they had not developed their own voice of authority. I recognized that some of them were grieving the loss of the way the church used to be. They remembered coming here, to the church of their childhood, safely held in their parents' opinions and ways of doing and being church. I found some of them still locked into those methods from as far back as the middle of the twentieth century.

Although the old ways of doing and being church worked beautifully in that era gone by, I knew that those rules no longer applied in the technologically advanced society in which we live today. This was hard news to deliver to the people who were holding this church together by threads. But, for their church to survive, they knew they needed to change. In my first five years at Wollaston, I relied heavily on leadership experts, including Ron Heifetz, who says that people do not resist change, but rather, they resist loss.[2] Although many describe the challenges of change in thinking, I found Heifetz's language of adaptive challenges and technical fixes to be readily applicable in my situation. I was clearly facing both, but most of what I saw then were adaptive challenges, which would take a long time to change. Quick fixes are pretty easy, but adaptive change involves grieving losses before setting foot onto new ground.

The members of Wollaston told me they were a friendly church. They may have been friendly to each other, but they did not understand the extravagant welcome they needed to extend to the new person, the stranger coming into the church. They longed to grow their church, but in their tight circle, I don't think they could really see beyond each other. I prayed for the fresh breath of the Holy Spirit to open their eyes and hearts. I was very clear that I had not come to be their chaplain or a hospice worker who would help them die. I had come to help them create a new church.

So, what did the members of Wollaston and I actually do? How did we begin to invite new people, the community, to come into the church? We made three leaps of faith during my first year at Wollaston that influenced how the people understood their relationship with the community around them. To begin to change the people, I knew we had to change the worship service.

I had only been at Wollaston for two months, May and June 2003, when I asked the leaders if we might change the Sunday morning worship service just for the summer to Wednesday evenings and hold the service in the church's social hall instead of the sanctuary. They agreed to try this, so I went about asking the people to make and serve a pot-luck supper each week, and I did some advertising to bring in people from outside the church. I called upon a number of my own musician friends to provide music in a variety of styles for the service. I offered participatory drama for the Scriptures and served Holy Communion as well. We did not worship on Sundays throughout that first summer nor did we return to Sundays for the next two summers.

This change was a big stretch for the people, but I also add-ed another program that pushed a few folks to complain. The program was called the "Church Mouse Luncheons: Under-standing My Neighbor's Faith," which I had very successfully run at my field education church each summer for the three years before I came to Wollaston. Phyllis Winslow, a mem-ber of that church, and I brought the program to Wollaston, and members from the congregation signed up to provide the luncheon. For four weeks in August, we organized a luncheon for the community and invited clergy and lay folks of various denominations to tell us about their faith journey and prac-tices. We heard from Mormons, Catholics, a Jewish rabbi, a Korean Presbyterian, and many others over the course of the month. These luncheons happened on Tuesdays, and then we had the potluck suppers and worship services on Wednes-day nights. I guess it was a lot to expect from them. But these luncheon, potluck suppers, and evening worship services were giving the members lots of opportunities to practice hospitality and to be an active and alive church. Although these first two programs lasted for only three years, a third one, the Healthy Kids Vacation Camp, a program for the wider community, is still thriving today.

I had some experience in writing successful grant proposals while working at several other jobs and thought that skill might help the church. I ran into one of my old colleagues, and we had a conversation about our church hosting a community event. Through her agency, we had an opportunity to apply for some grant money to do community children's programming, and our church had lots of space and that big stage. So, after developing the program we called "Healthy Kids Vacation Camp" on paper, she and I applied together for a grant. The money was used to pay a nutritionist and a yoga teacher to teach parts of the three-day camp that the church held during the public school vacation in February. We did receive that first grant and subsequent grants to run the program. Now we host more than fifty children from our church and the community for the camp at which everyone had and continues to have a great time each year.

The Wednesday night potluck suppers and worship service, the Church Mouse Luncheons, and the Healthy Kids Vacation Camp served the goal of bringing new people into our church. But I could feel tension building in the members as I continued to ask them to stretch themselves into these new community-oriented programs. Still, I believed strongly that if they wanted the church to grow, they had to work. I had turned up the heat, and some were not happy about that. I knew by their complaints that I might be pushing some too far and that I needed to have some pretty thick skin to survive. Initiating these three new programs in my first year at

Wollaston brought the community into the building and let people know this church was alive and welcoming and cared about the community. People became curious about our church, and some began to worship with us. From the first Healthy Kids Vacation Camp, two families, with five children combined, began to attend the church regularly and helped us begin a new Sunday school program. This is when I began to give a children's message in worship each Sunday.

The church continued developing children's programs. Super Kids Saturday, our next community outreach program, was organized by some members who could see and feel that things were changing and felt empowered and delighted to lead. More families came to the events, soon found their way into the worship service, and enrolled their children in Sunday school as well. We hired a student nurse (now a registered nurse) from the community to serve as our nursery care provider, and the younger children have been in her care on Sunday mornings for four years now.

Our children's programming has grown to at least five annual events, for which members of the church take more and more responsibility. As I write this, the church now has about thirty children in our Sunday school program and nursery, and we continue to grow through the outreach of our members. Parents in the church have started a Family Fun Night series in which they create free monthly church and community events for families in and around the church. As we continue to grow, I am diligent in supporting these leaders in the church. Now that we share the grassroots mission of evangelism, it is enlivening the spirit of worship in our church.

Another strategy for enriching worship has been to include visual art by teaching the cycles of the church calendar to both children and adults. The liturgical seasons are an integral part of our Christian heritage following the birth, life and ministry, death, and resurrection of Jesus Christ. The church calendar is familiar to congregations in some traditions, but it was new to some people at Wollaston, and worshipers needed a few years of cycling through the seasons before the rhythm began to become their tradition. But now, people anticipate them. They have become as natural as the seasons of spring, summer, fall, and winter. They hold memories, enliven the present, and point toward the future—last year, this year, and next year all at once. The liturgical seasons become foundational to faith formation, become a part of the history of the congregation, connecting us to the one body of Christ.

Images and themes of Advent, Christmas, Epiphany, Lent, Easter, and Pentecost now illuminate our sanctuary and nonverbally reinforce the cycle of events at the heart of the Christian calendar. These images help connect the worshipers with the mysteries of God. We are also developing a collective memory as our old congregation becomes new.

During that first year, we had to address the physical space in which we held our Sunday school. Our Christian education wing has two large classrooms and a nursery, all of which needed complete renovation. We had the walls painted in pastel colors and the floors cleaned, and we installed new ceilings in all three of these rooms and painted the hallway that connects them. As I said earlier, we did not have much money, so these renovations took a big chunk out of our dwindling treasury, but people were willing to take the risk to spend some money once they saw children coming to church. Our space became so beautiful that a community agency began to rent the nursery during the week. This produced some much-needed income for our church. Unfortunately, we found that we had to spend even more money to replace lead-painted windows in the rooms. We did that, too, however, and when all of these renovations were completed in 2004, we held a ribbon-cutting ceremony for the grand reopening and dedication of our Christian education wing. We even held our coffee hour in one of the classrooms on the dedication day. People began to feel a new sense of pride in what they had to offer, and I could feel their collective self-esteem beginning to rise. Having the number of children growing in our midst was making us more fully an intergenerational church. We were creating something new and not simply repeating the patterns of the past.

We had to build the Sunday school from the ground up. More people came to worship with their children. We made decisions about curriculum as we went along. We recruited more teachers and hired a Christian education director for five hours a week. As our Sunday school continued to grow, we hired one of our former seminarians as our minister of Christian education for twelve to fifteen hours per week. Eventually our one-room class grew to two, and this year I will teach a confirmation class. When our seminarian graduated, the parents and teachers stepped up to lead the children's Christmas pageant and to become more involved in teaching the story of the birth of Jesus to the next generation.

Field Education

Field education has given us the opportunity to hear multiple voices as worship leaders. Is there an example you might share about how one or more of our students have inspired you?

- As a trustee, at first I wondered how we would afford it, and now I feel that it's been so wonderful to have the students that we need more.
- The students' energy level is super and they try new things.
- I hadn't thought that I was being called by God to serve on the Teaching Parish Committee, but maybe I have.

The next big change was to figure out how to get more voices involved in worship leadership and to provide a model of shared leadership to the congregation. I looked to Andover Newton Theological School's Field Education Department. How could I continue to enliven worship, wake up the people, create a Sunday school program, write and deliver a children's message and an inspirational sermon every Sunday, and address all the other issues of this challenging and changing church? I needed help, and the church was in no financial position to hire an associate pastor.

And so, I prayed, and then I remembered that not long before I had been a field education student myself. I remembered my energy and enthusiasm when I was a student, and that I couldn't wait to lead worship and create community programs. So I contacted the field education department at my alma mater, Andover Newton Theological School, and enrolled in the supervisor's training course myself for the next year. I was allowed to have a student in the church while I did my training, but where would we find the three thousand dollar stipend the seminary required we pay the student?

Tom Clough, the area minister I mentioned in chapter 1, provided that answer. A church in West Newton, Massachusetts, had closed and sold its building. To continue its ministry, the congregation had decided to give away the money from the proceeds of the sale of the building. I applied for funding from the Central Congregational Church's Newtonville Legacy Trust, which funded our first seminary student, Jane MacIntyre.

As you can imagine, having a second voice in worship, someone who was eager to share the leadership with me, was a blessing to me and to the congregation. I spread myself even thinner in other areas of the church. Jane could preach and deliver lively children's messages. She offered a few new

programs in the church and helped to bring a new model to
our church, that of shared leadership.

I could feel God's hand in this because shortly after Jane
came to our church, I got a call from another woman, Cathy
O'Connell, a recent seminary graduate who was looking for
a church to be part of as she waited for a call to serve one of
her own. Tom Clough suggested that she call me and come to
learn about how we were growing a new church within our
old church in Wollaston. Cathy immersed herself in the congregation, getting to know the people one-on-one, and took
an active part in worship by reading the Scriptures. Many
Sundays she prepared and read explanations about the passages before the texts, inspiring in the congregation a real cu-
riosity about the Bible and a thirst to learn more. From what
I could gather, very little had been offered in the church in
the way of Bible study or adult Christian education for many
years. Most people were not comfortable in their knowledge
of the Bible. They were exhausted from doing what they
could to keep their church open. They needed the spiritual
nourishment of attending worship before they again became
ready to read the passages again. I am afraid that most of
them considered everything they did at the church as more
of a chore than service to God.

Over the course of the year Jane and Cathy spent with
us, I remember many from the congregation saying to me, "I
can't believe they wanted to come here! I guess we really do
have something to offer." Again, I felt the self-esteem of the
congregation rise as God's Holy Spirit enlivened this teaching ministry of our church. We continued to grow and began
to attract professional women to our congregation. Some are
retired and some work outside the home, but they all bring
a whole new energy to this community of faith. At the same
time, something was going on in the people in the original
circle: they were starting to look outward. They had begun to

loosen their grip on each other and were beginning to let the new people into the ever-widening circle. Ray Kinsella, the main character in *Field of Dreams*, heard a voice say, "If you build it, they will come." We were building, and they were coming!

The field education "project" of 2004 has continued. The church hosted our seventh student from Andover Newton Theological School in the 2008–2009 academic year. Each seminarian has been quite different from the others, each bringing his or her gifts and talents. One of our former students, Ann M. Aaberg, stayed with us two years beyond the one year of field education, when our church hired her to be our minister of Christian education while she finished her education and training at the seminary leading up to her ordination. In addition, several members of our church give extra support to each student through the Teaching Parish Committee (TPC) they serve on. And between continuous funding from the Central Congregational Church's Newtonville Legacy Trust and the Andover Newton Field Education Endowment Fund, we have gained so much. And it has not cost our church any money. In the past five years, we have applied for and received many such grants, which I will discuss in greater detail in the next chapter. My own theological underpinning when seeking funding is, "Never let money stop you from following one of God's good ideas." Field education and shared ministry are good ideas.

Music

We have been working with a variety of musicians and music styles and genres in worship. What has this been like for you? Will you share a highlight and a lowlight? Have you been affected by the introduction of PowerPoint in worship? Can you give an example?

Musical Style and Genre

- A lowlight for me was the music that Easter Sunday I had brought a guest with me and I was embarrassed by the music.
- A lowlight—miss the bigness of what we used to have here—three choirs back in the '60s. We used to be known all over the city for our music.
- I like the old hymns because that's what I was brought up on since I was six years old.
- A lowlight was when one of our musicians was repeating the same music within three months.
- A real highlight is our current Minister of Music, who is bringing vitality and spirit.

PowerPoint

- The PowerPoint doesn't excite me. I wish there were notes up on the screen.
- I find watching other worship services on TV boring compared to ours.
- At first, I was dead set against the PowerPoint, but I have seen that the music has improved and I feel that we are singing together and speaking as one body in our music. It is more of a corporate experience.

Up to 50 percent of the elements of worship can be musical. Several of the older members of our congregation nostalgically, and rightfully so, remember the days when the music of the church was exquisite. As children, they had grown up singing in the Bluebird Choir under the musical leadership of Ted Whittridge, who served as music director for thirty-plus years. The glory days of music are remembered fondly by those few in our church. In the 1990s church members took delight in purchasing a new Allen digital organ and had hoped to produce beautiful music again. Yet, while the desire for strong music programs is still palpable, these programs have not returned. In this old church, ghosts of the past linger in the air. I call it grief.

Five music directors led our worship music between 2003 and 2008. They ranged from reluctant church members to a very fine organist to a wonderful pianist. We learned a valuable lesson from this string of music directors with varying gifts: it cannot be assumed that because a person is a talented pianist or organist, he or she can direct, teach, or lead others in singing. Our current minister of music, Peter Johnston, is gifted in playing the organ, the piano, and the guitar. He also leads us in congregational singing. Today, our worship music is a blend of traditional and contemporary styles and includes children and adult voices as well as frequent guest musicians.

Through a generous grant from the Calvin Institute of Christian Worship Renewal Grant (funded through the Lilly Endowment) for the year 2007–2008, our church had the privilege to study with and learn from Thomas Long, who spent a full weekend with our congregation in September 2007. We have studied his book *Beyond the Worship Wars: Building Vital and Faithful Worship* with him and in small book discussion groups. Music in worship is so important that it emerged as the main topic in these study groups. Peter Johnston, our minister of music, engaged in several conversations with Tom on this topic. In the opening of his book, Tom writes about his visit to a congregation in an older church building, much like ours, where he was surprised to see a red drum set in the middle of the chancel. Our minister of music surprised Tom with a (borrowed) set of red drums in our sanctuary when he came to worship with us. Because so many of us had read this story in Tom's book, having the drums that day was fun for him and for us.

PowerPoint software, a projector, and a large screen were new features in our sanctuary. When one of our music directors introduced the method of projecting the lyrics on the screen, some members complained about the aesthetics of such modern technology in our Gothic Revivalist sanctuary. I did agree with them that the screen looked a bit out of place in our church, and eventually we figured out how to eliminate the screen by projecting the words onto a wall. Others complained that they needed to see the music as well as the words, so they continued to use the hymnals in the pews. However, now, after a few years of using this projection in worship, most of the people look up to see the words rather than down at the hymnals. A curious thing happens when the people look up to sing—you can actually hear them!

Although they were quite well hidden behind the pulpit on Sunday mornings, we did have a small choir when I first came to the church. Five women robed up each Sunday morning. Their seating arrangement was awkward because they faced the organ, not the congregation, to sing. Although the pulpit was just in front of them, I couldn't see them and barely could hear their soft voices. If I could not see nor hear them, neither could the congregation in the pews. Only after our third music director quit, I decided to take a different route with the music. Our church council agreed to take a break from both the traditional organ and choir to try something new—to have a pianist lead our congregational singing. We hired a young woman, who had never directed a choir, to play the piano for our worship services and to occasionally sing. Yes, I think some choir members were upset about that change, and some members were surprised that we were not using the organ they had purchased. But she brought us out of our routine of traditional hymns by introducing several praise songs, and she and her husband were the ones who actually introduced us to the technology of PowerPoint in worship. Unfortunately, she only stayed with us for a year.

Our church still does not have a choir. When the people ask me when we will have a choir again, I calmly tell them that I would like to have a choir, too. I tell them that we will have a choir when enough people step forward and say, "I want to be in the choir." Some former choir members would like to be in that new choir, but they need several stronger voices to help carry their sound out into the congregation. I believe that a new choir will emerge with a combination of old and new members when the time is right. Like a tulip bulb planted in the ground, this cannot be forced.

Five years of focusing on worship have produced good fruit. Hearing the children pray and sing in the church; reclaiming the Christian liturgical year in worship; extending an extravagant welcome to all guests; inviting multiple, talented worship leaders to add fresh energy to the service; and waiting for our choir to emerge have created a much healthier church. Worshiping God is the reason we gather on Sunday mornings, and now we believe our service reflects the love of God that we share.

There is tremendous competition from outside the church for the Sunday morning worship hour and fellowship time. The worship service must be excellent to engage people in corporate worship, not only to enhance their own everyday lives but also to nurture their spirits in the one body of Christ. As Christians, this is where we find our being and our hope of salvation.

When I think about the church neighbor who described our church by saying, "Oh, I thought that church was dead," I can safely say that the fruits of the Spirit are alive at Wollaston. She would not say that today, because now our church is the scene of more activity throughout the week than it had been for several decades. Our building is used every day by tenants who run children's programs and after-school dance classes.

When I came to Wollaston, I learned that the mission projects the congregation participated in were limited. Improving our worship service has brought us closer to the mission of Christ. A sure sign that our worship has led to a deeper sense of mission is that today we are participating in many mission projects. We don't have a youth group yet, but we provide overnight accommodations and hospitality to youth groups from across the country as they participate in mission projects all over the city of Boston. "Family Fun Nights" and Healthy Kids Vacation Camps are a mission we extend to the families of the wider community. Cub Scouts, Brownies, and Girl Scout troops meet weekly in our church. These are just a few of the programs that keep our lights on every day and into most nights of the week. Now we can say that our church looks alive because it is alive!

Chapter 3

Stewardship

The current financial crisis is, in fact, a spiritual crisis.
The problem lies less in parishioners' pocketbooks than
in their hearts and less in churches' budgets than in clergy's understanding of their members' lives.

—Scott Cormode, *Making Spiritual Sense*

The first thing I want to stress about stewardship is that a person's age affects how he or she views the matter. Financial contributions, or pledging, is the ground where generations clash, and age differences equal cultural differences. Those members of the church born before or into the middle 1940s grew up with the Great Depression mentality, either from their own experience or their parents'. The post-Depression years and World War II had a huge impact on the lives of these people all over the United States. Money was scarce, and people learned to save everything because they never knew when they would need it. People felt fear around the lack of resources, and a *culture of scarcity* permeated the thinking of these folks. That fear led to a pattern of holding on to everything from the smallest scrap of paper to rubber bands. Waste nothing.

In contrast, those called baby boomers, like myself, who were born between the end of World War II and into the early 1960s were raised within a *culture of abundance*. John F. Kennedy was the first president of the United States I personally remember. My generation lived through antiwar movements, the women's movement, and cultural shifts too numerous to name here. A new era ushered in the Woodstock generation, famous for sex, drugs, and rock and roll and other freedoms the people of just a generation before could scarcely imagine. These two mindsets, *scarcity* and *abundance*, are opposites, but they are both operating in churches today. In addition, the people born in the mid-1960s and later have grown up in an emerging technological society, with credit cards, expectations of a high-cost college education, and fantastic careers for everyone. This age group might be called the *throwaway culture*, because technology has advanced at such a rapid pace that soon after a digital camera or cell phone is massed produced, a new and better version is right behind it. Many of us now throw away the last one because we want to have the newest and most advanced technology at our fingertips.

Nipping at the heels of these generations are the children and youth of today. God help them, for theirs is a *culture of cleanup and creativity*, guided by the mantra "Recycle, renew, reuse." They face the challenges that some people have been trying to address for several decades: cleaning up the environment, finding renewable sources of energy, creating sustainable immigration policies in a global economy, finding a cure for cancer and for AIDS, and on and on it goes.

If your church is like Wollaston, then all four of these generations and mindsets are present in your congregation, too. I recognize that I am painting a very broad picture here. I do not underestimate the ability of some to mentally travel across the generations and hold a broader view of this cultural progression in order to create healthy stewards of all generations in the church. But I hope you will accept the terms I am using to understand how these differing perspectives affect stewardship and the meaning of money, buildings, and resources for the members of churches.

At Wollaston, technological advancements did not make it into the church in an effective way. As a result, I was puzzled by several things I noticed at my first meeting with the board of trustees—the stewards of the church's finances, buildings, and property. The moderator of the church was not present. Although term limits were specified in the church bylaws for all board positions, they were not observed. "Once a church officer, always a church officer" seemed to be the practice. The clerk of the church handled the agenda for the meeting and recorded the minutes. And perhaps most confusing of all, multiple, overlapping reports were distributed by those in attendance. Stapled to the agenda were a few beautifully crafted spreadsheets prepared by the clerk, who acted as an unofficial bookkeeper, listing lots of year-to-date data, including receipts and disbursements in nice, neat columns. The treasurer came to the meeting with only one little slip of paper, upon which two figures were handwritten. The first was the balance in the checkbook, and the second was how much money was needed to pay the remaining bills for the month. Another officer of the church, called the collector, passed out a financial income report for the preceding month. On the lined ledger paper was a handwritten report of all of the recent receipts for the previous month. At the bottom were the balances of the memorial fund account and the fuel fund account. (I later learned the policy of the church was that the collector kept track of all of the members' pledges and shared that information with no one else, not even the pastor. So I wondered what my role would be in making a connection between stewardship and faith, since I was not going to be privy to that information.) Another person who managed what they call the funds and legacies handed out one page, another difficult-to-read report.

At the time, I thought the church had a balance of about one hundred fifty thousand dollars in its treasury. I later learned that including the funds and legacies balances, it actually had a total of about two hundred fifty thousand dollars. Paying me would take a big chunk of that money, however. I wondered how I would help systematize the financial records and make them transparent, and how I would learn who pledged what so that I could do my pastoral work around stewardship. How could I help people understand the difference between confidentiality and secrecy? If I could not understand this system, I could not diagnose the problem, and so how could I initiate a cure? How could I move them to understand faithful, healthy stewardship when their own practices were locked up in an outdated, closed, antiquated, mom-and-pop system? Why weren't they taking advantage of secure and timesaving devices such as password-protected financial software and twenty-four-hour bank deposit boxes?

At least three issues needed to be addressed simultaneously. First, the disjointed reporting systems had to be updated. I was shocked that they had been able to function as long as they had within this disconnected system. It was as if each person were speaking and reporting in a different language. The reality is that a church is a small nonprofit business and Wollaston's financial practices needed to change to be effective in creating more transparency. I knew I needed to introduce small business practices into the church using computers and to help them identify and change some of the overlaps and gaps that existed within the individual reporting systems. By introducing the idea that other methods are available to choose from today, I could help the board of trustees and church officers streamline their practices. Some who had computer expertise were frustrated in trying to merge the past, present, and future practices. As a leader, I could educate and empower them to develop their own strategies and solutions for the adaptive challenges in our financial reporting system.

This was a necessary step so that we could then effectively record and communicate the financial information to the entire congregation. To develop a healthier church, we needed to enlist the rest of the congregation. We all needed a snapshot of the church's complete financial picture to understand better the urgency we faced of having only three years of operations money left.

The second issue was one of communication. The leaders were not clear who had access to what information and, by using computer-generated reports, how that information could be more widely shared with the congregation. I wondered how the board of trustees would react or respond to my messing with not just their financial system but also their positions as officers in the church. People who serve as church officers often have a high degree of commitment and emotional attachment to the service they provide for the congregation. Ministering to their feelings as change is implemented is as important as ministering to the financial health of the church. To me, it seemed very important to help them feel they were not being replaced.

A third issue of major concern to the trustees and needing to be addressed simultaneously was the dwindling funds. I began to think about theologies of stewardship. What did I learn in seminary about money that could help us now? I felt that I needed to talk to some people outside of Wollaston to understand how keepers of money in other churches operate. I had two conversations with two of the middle judicatory staff of our conference about church finances, and I learned that different churches have different mindsets about the church's money. Some, I was disappointed to find out, treat the church's money as if it were their own. One church in our own association held endowments of millions of dollars. When I asked them to lend us money, I was told, "We have money problems of our own." Another pastor was approached by our area minister for our denomination and asked to consider helping our church out. He was told right out, "Oh, that's not how we do business here." So, it wasn't just Wollaston that had money problems. These two churches, both with an abundance of money, are very generous in their mission giving, but they wouldn't even consider helping us, their sister church, as we struggled to survive. I guess I was naive.

At that time I felt we were on our own. I had not developed a theology of stewardship myself, so I went to my former professor from Andover Newton Theological School. Paul Adkins teaches church administration, and at graduation my class's valedictorian referred to him as "having a black belt in church administration." In a few short hours of discussion, he taught me two philosophies of stewardship, *docetic* and *incarnational*, that helped me to understand. The first method says Christians need to take care of only the spiritual; the other says we must take care of the spiritual *and* the material.

Doceticism, from the Greek *dokeo* ("to seem") teaches that Christ only *appeared* to be human; therefore, there was no incarnation and no divine Savior who died for sinners. Doceticism, a form of Gnosticism, which comes from *gnosis*, the Greek word for "knowledge," claims that Christ only *seemed* to die. *Incarnational theology*, on the other hand, embraces the life, death, and resurrection of Jesus Christ as told in the Gospel of John, which says that the Word became flesh and lived among us (John 1:14), and accepts that Christ is both fully human and fully divine. Adopting an incarnational theology would assume all aspects of humanity are included in ministry, including the material realities of buildings, property, and money. Therefore, an incarnational theology of church stewardship would include all aspects of both the spiritual and the material.

A quick way to think about the difference between these is this: "*Docetists* have clean hands; *Incarnationalists* get their hands dirty."[1] Perhaps some of my predecessors were of the docetic ilk, but I definitely needed to teach and model the incarnational at Wollaston. I had been getting my hands very dirty, and I had to help the congregation understand they had to take care of their building and money as part of the incarnational ministry of Jesus Christ, who we profess to believe was both human and divine. My responsibility, as I saw it, was to put some muscle and bone onto our collective response to Jesus's incarnation by moving out of the old theological practice of Docetism and into the theology the church has proclaimed for centuries.

I did not enter into deep conversations with my congregation or even with the trustees about what I had learned of Docetism and incarnational theologies of stewardship. The point, I felt, was for me to understand these distinctions. I didn't know exactly how long the church members had neglected the upkeep and maintenance of the building, but judging by the looks of some of the crumbling walls, inside and out, it had been decades. I wondered how long the congregation had been spending money without developing any way of building the treasury back up, but I knew we faced the worst financial crisis the church had ever known. Change would involve adaptive work and tending to the congregation's feelings. Some changes would be pastoral work that I should do. Their emotional ties to their teachers from the past were precious and yet were killing the church. I think their practices had become so ingrained that congregants could not see they were shortchanging themselves. Although their former beloved leaders taught them well in years gone by for a culture gone by, things had changed and, as a whole, the church had not kept up. It is understandable, and I am sure this happens in many churches.

Armed with my new understanding, I could teach by example an incarnational theology of stewardship—that we are responsible for the money, the buildings, and the grounds of the church. I don't think I ever used these words with the trustees, but I put this theology right into practice. Taking responsibility for the church's money, the buildings, and grounds may seem obvious parts of stewardship, but our congregation was struggling against some very poor odds. They were running out of money fast. Their building had been severely damaged by decades of water infiltration from rain and snow. The inside walls along one entire side of the building were crumbling. The odds were overwhelming that they could ever recover this beautifully crafted building. For as long as most of the trustees could remember, they had been in a financial struggle to do any upkeep or repairs to the building. It had simply gotten to be more than they could handle.

The condition of the building also spoke volumes to me about the hospitality issues of the congregation. Although the building, as I have said earlier, is an architectural gem, its true beauty could not be seen because of the lack of maintenance. How could the congregation welcome new people if the walls were crumbling, the floors weren't clean, and dust bunnies were everywhere? There were no signs inside the building to guide a potential visitor around. There was no schedule in place to ensure the regular maintenance of lawn care, trash removal, and snow and ice removal. These kinds of repair and maintenance issues, too, are part of stewardship. They are all part of caring for God's house.

It would have been easy for me to get discouraged, but isn't it true that when you trust God, something usually comes along that speaks to your heart? Such a thing happened to me when I felt overwhelmed by all the work that lay ahead of us. I was browsing through some church websites when I came across a pastor's letter to her congregation. The letter was written by Rev. Molly Baskette to the members of the First Congregational Church of Somerville, Massachusetts. She wrote of the challenges in redeveloping their church. In the letter, she pondered the question of how she would help the congregation develop their spiritual life, when, it seemed, in a flash of insight, she realized that stewardship is spiritual work. She announced, "This is our spiritual work!" That was what I needed to hear.

Folks in congregations are led into a deeper relationship with God, self, and others as they live into being good stewards of the finances, the buildings, and the grounds of their church and as they take on the challenges of the past to create a different future for the church. As Christians who believe that Jesus Christ was indeed both human and divine, our responsibility is to get our house in order. Not only must the members of Wollaston be prepared to do the ministry and mission work that we as a congregation are called to do as a part of the whole church of Jesus Christ, but also we are called to pass on this legacy to future generations. In so doing, we have to cross those cultural and generational barriers in our church, the mindsets of scarcity, abundance, throwing away, and cleanup and creativity.

My plans for leading the congregation into a healthier financial outlook began to unfold. First, we needed an intense focus on increasing the operational funds in our church. We did this through the annual stewardship campaign. Next, we would need to conduct a capital campaign that would create another fund to address the outdated heating system and allow us to begin assessing the structural damage to the building. We would need to find grantors to help with funding both the operations and these costly repairs. Having renovated the Christian education wing, the church needed to hire an appropriate staff to care for our growing nursery and Sunday school and a business administrator to oversee all of the space issues in the church, including rentals and repairs. Currently, we seem overstaffed for the size of our congregation, but we are still understaffed given the needs of a turnaround church. So, here is what we did.

Annual Stewardship Campaign and Capital Campaign

We have taken an extremely proactive role in annual stewardship campaigns and carried out a rigorous capital campaign. How has your proactive role been different for you from past practices?

Annual Stewardship Campaign

- We did the same thing year after year and got into a rut that we never get out of.
- Being proactive is the way to go. In the past, stewardship was never mentioned, and we had to face up to the reality of our situation.
- Our former ministers were not strong on stewardship.
- It is horrifying to me that people don't pay attention to how much the cost of running the church has gone up.

Capital Campaign

- I was against hiring the consultant and spending all that money, but as it evolved, I loved the Capital Campaign.

Wearing the hard hats in worship made it fun; seeing posters about it all around the church was fun. You never knew what was coming next. The committee made it fun for everyone

- When you say we need to raise a half a million dollars, that seems impossible, but five hundred thousand seems possible.
- The difference is that you [pastor] have hope.
- Whenever I have extra money, I think, "Oh good! I can give it to the church."

People who attend 12-step programs often say, "If you do what you always did, you're going to get what you always got." Wollaston had followed the same patterns in their stewardship campaign for years. Perhaps you will recognize this approach. One member gives a financial giving testimony to the congregation in worship. Someone else writes a letter telling the reasons she gives to the church and in the same letter asks each member to make his or her financial pledge based on faith and ability. This had been the traditional approach at Wollaston.

So, in my first year, we inserted a couple of little new twists in an effort to start doing things differently. Three people were asked to give their testimonies in the worship service about why they give to the church. The letter went out but with some newly created materials, borrowed with permission of the writer, John Hamilton of the First Congregational Church United Church of Christ in Norwood, Massachusetts, inviting the people to look at stewardship as their "soul responsibility." These materials explained that stewardship is a spiritual matter. A puzzle was used as a metaphor for our combined pledges, and people were invited to be pieces of the puzzle. Pledges went up considerably that first year, and we continue trying out new twists on the annual campaign.

Another example of a new twist occurred in 2007 when an elderly member of the congregation died and her family gave the church a sizable sum of money. We put half of it right into the general fund and the other half into the capital campaign, and then we asked the congregation collectively to match the other half of her gift in their pledge to the general fund for the year. We considered her gift "Pennies from Heaven" and played that song in her honor on Stewardship Sunday. In the next five years, the members' contributions more than doubled. The small circle of members has quadrupled and as a new congregation has taken root in their midst, more people are contributing to the financial well-being of the church. Still, stewardship education had been sorely lacking in our church for decades, and in both new church starts and turnaround churches, membership is known to grow at a faster rate than pledges. Although our congregation continues to grow in members and spiritual vitality, we continue to run our budget at a deficit. We rely on the generosity of outside sources for funds to supplement our budget until our pledging catches up to our budgetary needs. So the work of stewardship education continues.

I have also needed to convey the message that repairing and preserving the building for future generations is essential. Since the building was neglected for so long, repairs would also be very costly, too much for our small congregation to carry. At this time, we have raised enough money to repair and maintain the heating system, and the repairs on the building are far more substantial. But our church leaders have also been communicating a positive message: we have been creating a new church for those who are not yet there. Those few current members who were active in 2003 know that they are part of this rebuilding and not just making a comfortable place for themselves. They, as well as the newer members, are charged with figuring out what changes will be

life sustaining for the future of this church into the generations to come. In New England churches heat is a necessity,
and our building, for both its size and its architectural significance, is a tremendous asset to the wider community. Using
our building for the purpose of connecting with that wider
community has enriched the vitality of our congregation.

Although the congregation had raised the money to
purchase a new organ in the 1990s, Wollaston had not con-
ducted a capital campaign since 1962, when the church built
the Christian education wing. That was over forty-five years
ago and was done by the previous generation. So none of the
present members knew how to go about conducting a capital
campaign. I went to our conference's stewardship associate,
and he gave me names of some campaign consultants. After
several interviews, the church hired a former clergyman who
had helped many churches run successful capital campaigns.
Hiring a consultant was a substantial cost to us, but the congregation agreed that as difficult as it was to do so, we had to
spend money.

The consultant asked me to invite six members of the
church to be on the committee. Everyone, myself included,
was taken aback at the amount of work the campaign required. One member's reaction to our task stands out in my
mind: "You mean we have to ask the people face to face for
money? We've never done that before."

Throughout the campaign we kept the congregation
informed by giving weekly updates during worship. Committee members wore hard hats with our names on them,
making some fun out of the seriousness of our situation. We
came very close to reaching our financial goal and allocated most of the funds for an updated heating system for our
church. Our campaign contributions were collected over a
period of three years. When the campaign concludes, church
leaders hope the congregation will reallocate the money they

were giving to the capital campaign to increase their annual pledge to the general operations fund of the church.

The campaign has had a positive effect on the congregation. Many were surprised that we could raise the money, and it also showed members' commitment to the church's future. Because the heating system is so old, we had to hire specialists to understand the complex pneumatic operations system. Because of our building's historic and architectural significance, it was accepted onto the National Register of Historic Places in 2008. The Massachusetts Historical Commission granted us matching funds and we hired an architectural firm to assess the water damage to the building and to draw the plans for its repair. Our architect is also collecting professional estimates for these repairs and helping us understand which grants we might apply for to finance these costly repairs. We are looking at a five hundred thousand dollar cost for the restoration of the building. Not only are we turning the church around but we are also making it useful for generations to come. The commitment of our congregation to increased financial giving has improved the outlook for future ministry.

Grant Writing and Resource Development

Grant writing and resource development have played a significant role in our church turnaround process. Can you name a time when you were challenged in your thinking or actions about money and church? Can you give an example of your own increased financial giving or that of someone you know who has increased his or her financial giving?

- Churches are just quietly fading away without asking for help, without making a spectacle of themselves.
- We never even thought of grants.
- I had never heard the word grant before. We were a self-

supporting church and to my knowledge, we never looked outside the church. There is a pride in this church that we can take care of ourselves. It was almost shocking to think about asking somebody else to help us out. It wasn't just welfare, but there are actually organizations out there who would give money to help spread the Christian message. That makes it a different thing.

In our church and in the tradition of the United Church of Christ, each church is self-governing and financially independent, save special contributions to specific funding for the wider church and mission. From what I understand, grant writing is a relatively new endeavor for churches and has come about as a result of decline in most mainline Protestant churches. Grant writing had been part of several of my former jobs, so it was a natural approach for me to take in seeking funds for the church. This is a possibility that I hear many churches are exploring as their treasuries diminish. I was asked to lead a workshop for our conference two years ago and learned from the thirty-five attendees that they were looking for grants for reasons similar to ours at Wollaston. The top two financial priorities in these New England churches were money to repair their buildings and money to increase their staff.

In chapter 2, I described the first grant proposals we wrote to fund the field education student and for the first Healthy Kids Vacation Camp. Since then we have written and received many more grants, some larger and some smaller. The grants have been a huge part of our turnaround. Getting those first grants showed the congregation we could write successful grants and that people outside the congregation believed Wollaston could do valuable work. We learned that *grants* a small amount of money could make a huge impact on our congregation and community.

Grant writing is a technical skill, but there is also an art to the process. I had honed my own skills from writing several grants in my previous job as a community coordinator and began to enlist help in writing from several members of the congregation. To date, we have received from various sources more than two hundred thousand dollars in grants—what it has cost to turn the church around. The largest grants have come from our denomination. The national setting of the United Church of Christ granted us money from the New and Renewing Churches Endowment Fund. The Massachusetts Conference of the United Church of Christ, the conference to which Wollaston belongs, granted us funds through the Commission for Evangelism and Church Vitality. We did not receive either of these two grants, however, until after the third year of the stabilization of our church, after we had shown significant growth and promise in membership and money.

We have applied annually to several local sources that partially fund our children's community programs. Our congregation was a 2007–2008 recipient of a grant from the Calvin Institute of Christian Worship, which received its funding from the Lilly Endowment. We have recently received funding to launch a Pastoral Residency for Turnaround Ministers in which we will train new pastors to lead turnaround work in other churches.[3] The funds also cover the development of a seminary course called "Turnaround Ministry," which could, ideally, become a component in Master of Divinity degree programs.

These grants have provided our congregation with money for the operations of the church, including supplementing salaries, and for community outreach programming. We

have received additional funding from the area association
of our denomination to cover the costs of researching and
obtaining funding from local, state, and national grantors for
our historic building restoration project.

To describe the overall effect that receiving these multiple
grants has had on our congregation, I need to talk separate-
ly about the old congregation and the newer congregation.
These grants have provided older members much relief from
feeling that they had to do everything themselves. They have
enjoyed the peace of knowing help was available to them.
The grants have extended the life of the old church while the
new church is being created.

As I nurture the newer members in the church, I struggle
with several issues. The newer members are the ones who
will ultimately sustain this church by building up the mission
and the ministry for future generations; therefore, it seems
unfair to ask them to also pay for the years of decline. The
damage to the building happened long before they came to
the church, so I don't know if it right to ask them to pay to
fix it. I am curious as to what other people think about this.
When the church had only a few new members, the older
members decided to invest some of the remaining money to
renovate the Christian education wing on the faith that more
children would be coming. One long-term member said:

*Part of the challenge for me was putting money into
something you don't know if it's going to work. If you do
the math, we have spent about one thousand to fifteen
hundred dollars per child in these renovations. When my
child was here in Sunday school, we did not spend any
money on the Sunday school. Now that child does not
even want to come to church. That was a time we were
not investing in our own children. We were so afraid of*

spending money. Now the new children are learning and
they will have something to take with them. We have to
make room for the new kids.

The money spent has increased our hospitable space for families with children in Sunday school and has also resulted in our receiving rental income from the space during the week. Growing the church has also included adding new staff positions to oversee these operations. We have slowly been moving to a professional team model for our church staff. I have been reminded many times that other churches use mostly volunteer laypeople to run the church. But the systems of our church were broken and needed professional development to create healthy operations to meet today's culture.

Staffing the Turnaround Church

We have spent a significant amount of money on renovating the Christian education wing of our building. This has led to both growth in our Sunday school and our hiring a Christian education minister and nursery care provider. We have also needed to hire a business manager to coordinate building rentals and space scheduling, which meant also increasing the hours of custodial maintenance to the building. Can you share how you first felt about spending money on these renovations and creating new jobs, and then can you give specific examples of how you feel about these actions that have enhanced the growth and vitality of our church?

- We are Yankee conservatives here and closed with a dollar. We have now changed direction! Holding on to money, I knew the outcome; but doing this, spending money, I didn't know what the outcome would be. So, why not? We would have hit the wall and that would have been the end of it, so why not try a different road?

- You have got to spend money to make money. I feel good that we have a place to provide a nice, new space for people.
- Parents aren't going to bring their children to a place that doesn't meet their family's needs. In fact, we have lost families in the past because we didn't have a program that met their children's needs.
- You renovated my thinking!

When I was hired as the first full-time pastor of Wollaston in several decades, the church had only one other employee, the church secretary, who worked part time. An older teenager was paid to do minimal maintenance, such as vacuum the sanctuary, change light bulbs, wash the floor of the social hall, and put out the trash. Because we were taking serious, ambitious action about the future of the church, we had nowhere near the number of staff we needed. You might find it curious that we hired people to do what many small- to medium-sized congregations have done with volunteer labor. I mentioned earlier that the few members who hired me were exhausted from holding the church together for a long period of time. Many of them needed some relief. And although some of them stepped up their involvement, most of them had been wringing their hands about how to grow their church. They either did not have the energy or the skills readily available to oversee building coordination, to coordinate space rentals, to lead a new Sunday school program, or to provide the repairs and maintenance of the building and grounds. These are the reasons we needed to add paid staff to establish positions that, when we are a larger and healthier church, lay volunteers may want to assume.

Several years into my ministry at Wollaston, Tom Clough—the same Tom Clough who had told me in 2003

that Wollaston was at the bottom of the list of churches—
told me with amazement that we now had the largest staff
of all the churches in the Metropolitan Boston Association!
Improved financial practices, healthier business and administrative practices, new building income, and grants had all
contributed to our ability to pay for this larger staff.

Turnaround ministry might be more work than many
pastors and congregations want to or are able to undertake.
In 1993 George Barna wrote about several unique character-
istics of turnaround church pastors in his book *Turn-around
Churches: How to Overcome Barriers to Growth and Bring
New Life to an Established Congregation.*[2] Unfortunately, I
only recently came across this book or it might have helped
me a great deal along the way. For example, I was intrigued
by the attributes of a turnaround pastor he identified: youth,
workaholism, spiritual commitment, strong personality,
and potential visionary leader. In chapter 1, I wrote that one
my own attributes is that I am a terminal optimist. Maybe I
should also have included the other traits Barna listed (with
the exception of youth). Barna's research showed him that
no one over age forty-five was considering this turnaround
work and that the majority of turnaround pastors are in their
thirties and forties. He also says that most pastors have only
one turnaround in them and do not generally go to a second
turnaround church.

Without exploring all the attributes Barna lists, I will tell
you a story that illustrates the workaholic trait in me, a story
that also explains our congregation's decision to hire more
staff. As a new pastor, I was trying to keep up with all of my
new responsibilities. The work of worship planning, getting
to know my new congregation, and understanding some
of the dynamics that were preventing them from growing
would have been enough work for anyone. But all that was

compounded by five funerals within my first two months, learning more and more about my new role, and trying to do everything the members asked of me. I was also trying to develop an understanding of the congregation's expectations of me.

The truth was that I was physically and emotionally exhausted. Within several weeks, I had finished three years of theological school, gone through graduation, been ordained by my association, and started my call at Wollaston. The daily responsibilities of a pastor were overwhelming me.

I carried on the best I could, holding up okay, or so I thought, until the Sunday afternoon I went to the open house at the local food pantry. By that time I was already pooped from the morning at the church, but a member had asked me to go to this event and, dutifully, I obliged. I remember that I had trouble finding a parking space, so I parked on a side street. I locked my car and started to cross the street. By the time I reached the middle, my whole body was leaning to the left, but momentum kept me moving forward as I fell on my left side. When I finally hit the ground, I was half on the sidewalk and half onto someone's lawn. It was not a pretty picture. I just wanted to lie there and cry until I fell asleep. But I didn't. Mentally, I scanned my body and assessed that I hadn't broken any bones, got up, and brushed myself off, continuing on as if nothing had happened. Talk about denial! I put a smile on my face and entered the food pantry for its open house.

Although I had a smile on my face for everyone, on the inside I knew something was wrong. I had just taken on way too much, more than I could handle and my body was telling me to slow down. I had to get help. I didn't come to this church to kill myself, and what kind of example was I setting by taking on too much? I had to face the tension I felt between the pain and possibility of this church. I had to delegate responsibilities, which meant adding more staff, because the congregation felt too fragile to ask members to do any more. I was not the savior of this church. I was also not going to be a martyr by driving myself into the ground. So, how did we increase our staff and distribute so much responsibility?

Wollaston hired staff before our members' financial giving started to increase by using more of the dwindling funds and by adding more rental income to the church. The church secretary continued to do the office administration, but we hired a part-time business manager to deal with all of the building and space issues. We hired a part-time custodian to do regular maintenance, and I enlisted members—volunteers—to start some of the deep cleaning. We hired a part-time Sunday school director to oversee the Sunday school and nursery, and we hired a Sunday morning nursery care provider. Someone needed to help me with worship leadership, and in came our first seminarian. All of these people helped take a piece of the workload of the church, and I got to work helping the members get unstuck from the past. I will say more about how I worked with the leaders in the next chapter, but I had to help them acknowledge realities of the present and infuse more hope for the future. We needed to start thinking long term.

One member described our decisions to hire a larger staff saying, "We are not spending money, we're investing it!" And, indeed, we were. We were investing in the future of the church, investing in the ministry and mission of Jesus Christ. Another member said, "Originally, I was against the renovations of the Christian education wing, because I thought we were throwing good money after bad. I thought that the church would not last and that a developer would come in and tear down the building. But now, with the grants coming in and the people coming in, I know the church will not close."

With the stories of how worship and stewardship have been transformed, I will now turn to the third topic crucial to turnaround church ministry, that of leadership. Changes in leadership were hardest for some of the people, who eventually decided to leave the church. Some of the less vocal members began to voice their opinions, which seemed to challenge those who had assumed positions of authority. Several confrontations demonstrated that everyone had some very difficult decisions to make. Although the future of the Wollaston church was dependent on God, it became clear that our work had just begun. The vision of a new church would only become a reality if we were willing to pray and work for it. In the next chapter, you will see that not everyone agreed with this approach.

Chapter 4

Leadership

Trust is a rope, long in the braiding.
—Robert Smyth, "You're Welcome"

What kind of leader does it take to bring a congregation from the arid wilderness to cool water and refreshment? What sort of leadership would allow the members of our congregation to have hope? Strong, solid leadership proved to be the third binding agent, along with worship and stewardship, that has given the members of Wollaston confidence to wade deeply into the waters of change. In this chapter, I will talk about my own leadership, the leadership among the members of the church, and leadership from our denomination, the United Church of Christ, that have brought this refreshment.

I will begin with a story about myself. About ten years ago I began working for a nonprofit agency as a community coalition coordinator for the city of Quincy's Tobacco Control Program. As part of a community empowerment project, our staff invited about twenty people from the community to take part in a leadership-training program. The facilitator for the day was Julio Rodriguez, a community

organizer flown in from Chicago especially for the training. As the day progressed, people began working in small
groups, and I dove into one of the groups as a member. I was
having a grand old time when one of my colleagues took my
elbow and gently pulled me out of the group. He said, "You
already know how to do this. This is about them learning to
do it. Let them learn." I had to step back. This was a valuable lesson for me to remember when, as a new pastor, I was
called both to lead people and to nurture and develop leaders
in the congregation.

After decades of decline in the Wollaston church, I began
my watch with a core group of people who had spent their
time and energy trying to keep the church afloat. Although
138 people were listed as members on the church roster, not
even one quarter of them came to worship on Sunday mornings. The years of wear and tear showed everywhere. As hard
as they had worked, stagnation had set in, creating an aura of
hopelessness. They knew their church would die soon—unless they changed. But as tired as they were, some still had
a heart for the mission of Christ in this church. I needed to
assess the strengths and weaknesses of the congregation and
its leaders. They were limited by their small numbers and
dwindling financial resources. But I did not know if they had
looked outside their membership and the church for help.
One of their strengths was that most of them were willing to
try new things. They were eager to embrace new and creative
leadership, or so I had been led to believe. They had a desire
to move forward and to get their own creative juices flow-
ing. I learned that my first impressions about the congregation's denial didn't really apply to everyone. Some members
seemed to be more flexible in their thinking and had potential as leaders of change. They were interested in reaching out
for help and resources from our denomination, the United

Church of Christ, and I felt that their hope, although quiet, was still alive.

Those who initially presented themselves as leaders did not represent the whole congregation. And the methods of governance that had led this church to stagnation appeared to be controlling the church's direction. Congregants seemed to feel a sense of loyalty and gratitude toward the people who had stepped up to keep the church going. But stepping up under those adverse conditions does not necessarily constitute genuine leadership. There was a definite sense of who was an insider and who was an observer, as this family church maintained secrets and long-standing patterns characteristic of a closed community.

As a psychologist, I was prepared to look below the surface to see if I could find where the strings were attached and who pulled them. I needed to discover where the power of this church was centered. Were ghosts of deceased relatives, the once-full choir loft, the memories of children singing, and other mental images of an era gone by lingering in the air? Those in positions of leadership seemed tied to a past that could prevent them from leading change. I knew that it would take time to help people deal with all the loss and change they had been experiencing, but we did not have much time. This gave them a sense of urgency, something essential to our successful and life-sustaining change. Leading the congregation through change would challenge that which many held dear, their loyalties to the past.

I also had to learn what rate of change would be tolerated and then set the pace. Some say it can take as long as five years for members of an established congregation to develop trust in their pastor. We did not have five years, so I had to earn their trust much more quickly. I love this line from a poem by Robert Smyth: "Trust is a rope, long in the braiding." Not all of them trusted me to lead, but some told me later that they felt doing something was better than doing nothing.

While I assessed the state of the congregation, I needed to keep in mind the fact that the work of a turnaround pastor is demanding physically, mentally, emotionally, and spiritually. To lead this kind of transformational work, you must stay fit in all of these areas. Serving as an effective pastor in a church today has been described by church consultant and author Lyle E. Schaller as at least three times harder than it was in 1955.[1] As a turnaround pastor, I believe the work is possibly five or more times harder than that. Why? In the turnaround church, every system of the church is subject to review, reappraisal, and change. This is daunting enough, but perhaps what makes all of this work even more difficult is pastoring the people of the old church while simultaneously building the new church. Recent thinking at the judicatory level about turnaround churches suggests a new approach to this dilemma: to send two pastors to a turnaround church. One would serve as a chaplain to the older congregation and perhaps work only about ten or twelve hours per week. The second pastor would specialize in building the new church. As I grow further into my call and role as a turnaround pastor, I have come to think the title "church recovery specialist" appropriately describes the work of a turnaround pastor. As more and more mainline Protestant churches find themselves in various stages of decline today, clergy and laity need to constantly develop new models to help congregations assess their options. I have said to many that a turnaround pastor needs two things, thick skin and stretch pants! You need both because it is not always clear if the people are biting you or feeding you. Some will do both. Self-care and outside support are crucial.

Spiritual directors, mentors, and therapists can be very helpful for the turnaround pastor when sorting out multiple dysfunctions in church systems. Fortunately for me, the Massachusetts Conference of the United Church of Christ had received funding from the Lilly Endowment for a Sustaining Pastoral Excellence Program through which newly ordained clergy were mentored by a seasoned pastor for the first three years of their ministry. As a new pastor, being in a small group of my peers, all new clergy, and being mentored by Judy Brain, a seasoned pastor of more than twenty-five years, provided tremendous support and encouragement as I began to lead the turnaround at Wollaston.

Church Governance and Leadership

Eight months after my arrival at Wollaston, a significant change in the church governing body occurred. We suspended the large executive board and made room for a new church council. After a trial period, the church council was voted in as the method of church governance to continue. Some members disagreed with this change or felt left out of the new governing body and consequently left the church. Can you describe specifically how you felt about both of these things, and, in hindsight, how the church council has led our church in a positive direction for growth and vitality?

- The Church Council was definitely the way to go. I hated going to those old Executive Board meetings of twenty-two people. Things got tabled for three or four or five months at a time. With the six-person Church Council, we could react faster and get things done quicker. Meeting twice a month helped to make changes fast and furious. We stayed focused, kept our eye on the ball.
- The new leadership allowed the change to begin. The church was returned to the congregation. Before only a few people did all the work and we allowed that to happen. Now, the people got their church back. The transition was smoother than it might have been.

> - We've gone from dark and gloomy to light and bubbly! In hindsight, I think it was the development of the Church Council that drew the line between the past and the future.

It did not take long for quieter members to speak to me about some deeper issues of concern. Because I was hearing different versions of the same stories, I knew that complications in leadership were bound to occur. Early on, I suspected there were those who could and would make it difficult for a new leader to become established. Their resistance to change did, in fact, lurk right below the surface.

I sought help from our area minister when I faced a power struggle with one particular group in the church, the trouble I had sensed was lurking. This group seemed to have its own leader, and it wasn't me. I needed to confirm my assessment with a trusted colleague. In so doing, I realized this smaller group had to be confronted in order for the rest of the congregation to be freed from its control. Several people in this group had been on my search committee, so they had once supported me, but after six months they were trying to undermine me. It is hard to say why. I don't think it was personal. At least I told myself that. Behind the scenes, however, they were making phone calls to other members, trying to rally support against me. There was not one specific thing that I did or said that offended them, but I think they were angry because I was not falling in line as they had expected I would. I think they liked things the way they were, with themselves in charge, and I represented a challenge to them. When these leaders finally left the church, they were successful in taking several members with them; but others, who had previously been under the thumb of these leaders, were finally able to freely express their own voices.

Following the departure of these unhappy members, we felt a little giddiness in the air as the rest of the people began thinking and talking for themselves. Ensuring the survival of the church suddenly became their job, and they were excited about the task. They began talking to each other and reclaimed their own authority as members. They had also given me the authority to lead their congregation. I found that in a turnaround church, where conflict and change can go hand in hand, it was important for me to continually remember what I had been trained and called to do. Sometimes my call became cloudy. In seminary I had been trained to lead worship, to administer the sacraments of the church, and to give pastoral care. But in reality, the people of Wollaston had also called me to lead them through the rocky waters of change. In that process, I was challenged.

One issue I needed to address was that the church's executive board was too big to be effective. Of the twenty-five active members, twenty-two were on this board. The group found it difficult to come to any decisions or to take any action. I didn't know much about different models of church governance and neither did the members. So we got some advice from our area minister about how to go about dismantling the executive board to try something that would be more effective for us. Two members accompanied me to meet with Tom Clough. He suggested a model that included a church council of six people, which would be a more appropriate number for the size of our congregation at that time.

The executive board then called a meeting of the congregation to make this proposal. On that evening a few church members helped me set up the church's social hall with several rows of chairs before the meeting was to begin. We had put a few chairs at the front of the room for the speakers who were expected to talk about the proposal. But what happened next really surprised me. One of the people, whom others had viewed as a leader and who eventually left the church, came into the hall and began setting up tables and taking the chairs we had already set up and putting them around the tables. I asked him to stop and said that we had already set up the room the way we wanted it. He got very angry with me and refused to stop what he was doing. I insisted that he stop. Others were in the room when he raised his voice to me and stormed out of the room. He did not return that night. I was stunned by his behavior but grateful that others had witnessed his outburst. He eventually did apologize to me for his disrespect, but he left the church within months after that incident.

At the meeting, the clerk of the church outlined what a church council would look like. Tom answered questions about the proposed new structure. By the end of the meeting, the congregation had agreed to ask me to select six people based on their length of membership in the church to serve on the council. Two very long-term members, two midterm members, two newer members, the clerk of the church, and I would make up the proposed council. Each of us, excluding the clerk, would have one vote on church matters. In this way the congregation began to develop a practice of shared leadership among the church council members and the pastor. The meeting went forward and the congregation agreed to bring this new council initiative to the annual meeting for a vote. The council was approved, we suspended the bylaws for a year, and this new council met twice a month for the next two years. I did not ask any of those folks whom I knew were bad-mouthing me to be on the council.

Not everyone in a turnaround church is going to agree with the way change happens. Power struggles and conflict need to be dealt with in calm and systemic ways. Fortunately for us, we had the support of our area minister and

new leaders to manage our conflict. Previously,
had lived with two major fears. The first was t
would close, and the second was that those wh
would leave. The second came true and oth
up to lead. Yes, those who had threatened to leave did. vv...
those who remained saw their worst fear come true and they
survived, they felt free to change direction. The result of that
group leaving was a shared leadership that set the stage for
dramatic change. Members took responsibility as a spiritual
community for worship, stewardship, and leadership. The
congregation took a new look at itself and invited the Holy
Spirit to fill the vacuum created by its former leaders' departure. The Spirit creates an environment where people can
take initiative to empower themselves and others, take risks,
and experience success.

Successfully shifting the responsibility to lead from one
small group to the entire congregation was an exhausting
process. Part of what made it so tiring for me was that I was
the one being blamed by the people who left. I was the one
who heard about the phone calls they were making to dis-
credit me. I tried to keep a calm head, but inside I felt hurt.
What was my call again?

With congregation members feeling empowered, we were
being equipped to discern the mission and ministry of our
church. The people had found their voices for a reason, to
serve God. The responsible course of action for me as the
pastor was to be responsive and to provide a nonanxious
presence as the new church council did its work of restruc-
turing the church. Long-standing committees were disband-
ed and renovations began. It took a two-ton dumpster to get
rid of all that stuff in the closets. This kind of action-oriented
leadership began to bring in fresh air, and the people began
to feel better about tackling some of the problems that had

.evented growth and vitality in the church. We initiated an annual Rake and Pray Day at the church to keep up with this kind of deep cleaning. After about three years, we got most of the heavy cleaning done.

At times I wondered if I was doing the right thing in leading members to disrupt the old governing rules and patterns of leadership. I felt a moral and spiritual commitment to do what was right on behalf of the people, but when almost half of the congregation left the church, I must admit I doubted myself. But those who remained did step up and take personal responsibility for the church's new direction and they deepened their commitment to the church. The heartbeat of the Spirit grew stronger.

That heartbeat was made manifest in often surprising ways. For example, the members had previously thought of themselves as a church family. This is not always a healthy thing, because when dysfunction is present, it takes time for a congregation to move out of that enmeshed thinking. It took time for other lay leaders to accept their role and to listen carefully to the feelings of other members. Once the feelings were expressed, the positive side of change involved thinking through new strategies and developing action plans. As their pastor, I spent time listening to members' feelings about their perceived loss, their grief, and their fears, but the new church council needed to get busy with finding ways to move the congregation to healthier ways of congregational life.

The church council met twice a month for two years with perfect attendance by everyone. Council members' commitment to change was palpable. By the third year of the council, it only met once a month. The council was not intended to be a permanent governing body, but rather a temporary bridge to get us from here to there, wherever *there* is. But by the fourth year, nearly all the church business seemed to be coming to the council. I think this was a natural consequence of the design, but it was also the clue that the time had come to branch out the leadership and develop yet another governing system. The flaw in the system was that it did not take into account that dismantling the old board and committee structure would necessitate establishing new boards and committees. Those groups, which we now call teams, have evolved to address the needs of the significant growth of our congregation. The council thought taking a time-out to reassess the needs of the congregation would be a good thing. A temporary system that included the church council and the deacons was put in place to make any major decisions on behalf of the church while the congregation developed the next system based on the church's many changes.

After the congregation had worked on stabilizing the church for the first three years of my ministry at Wollaston, the conference sent us two vitality coaches, Paul Nickerson and Jim Griffith, whom you will read about later in this chapter. They affirmed that we had stabilized our church, turned it around, and had moved into the next phase of turnaround called "new church start." We were ready to have the coaching these two experienced pastors and coaches could provide. As you can imagine, the needs of a new church start are very different from those of a dying or revitalizing congregation. Some might say that we as a congregation, and Jim and Paul agreed, were in the midst of an identity crisis. They helped us to understand this as a normal part of our church's recovery. During the period we changed our governance for the second time, Paul and Jim had become familiar names and faces in our church.

Over the next year several retreats and many planning meetings were held. The congregation participated and all were kept informed by what came to be called the retreat planning committee, and everyone continued to give their input. A proposal was put forth to the congregation at the annual meeting in January 2009. We settled on a three-pronged model of leadership we called Stewards. This system of governance, which we are currently using, has two stewards of worship and education, two stewards of mission and outreach, and two stewards of building and resources. Of course, we also have elected officers of the church, a moderator, a clerk, and a treasurer, legally required for a nonprofit organization such as a church.

You might wonder how governing by stewards is different from the former church council. If you imagine a triangle consisting of three triangles, each with many smaller triangles in it, you will have a visual image of this system. The three main triangles are color coded for easy identification. One of the main functions of each pair of stewards is to create communication loops between the stewards and members of the congregation around their areas of responsibility. So, for example, the stewards of worship and education check in regularly with our worship team, the Sunday school team, the liturgical arts team, and so forth. The stewards of mission and outreach are responsible for communicating with the members who organize and run outreach programs of the church, such as the Family Fun Night team. Publicity, church publications, and media also fall under the resources stewards. The stewards of building and resources meet with our grant writers, building repair consultants, and financial team. Since this is still a new system to us, we anticipate we will have bugs to work out along the way; but for now, we expect that the three steward pairs may only need to meet together four or five times a year. Officers of the church will meet with the stewards as needed. It may take us some time to determine the best ways to communicate, but we are working on ways to do that.

Our congregation believes this governing system fits our church as it has evolved and grown over the past five years and that it will continue to empower members to create and lead programs and projects of their design. This governing system is designed to meet the diverse needs of at least four generations in the church. Today's congregation reflects a diversity of religious backgrounds and so we are striving to find ways that unify us. We agree that leadership and governance are not permanent structures, and that change in both from time to time is healthy. Change has been written on our hearts.

Community Outreach Programs

Many new outreach programs have been developed in the past five years. The community children's programs have directly contributed to growth of our church and increase in worship attendance. It takes many volunteers to make these programs excellent. Can you give an example of a time when you participated in the planning and implementation of any of these programs? What was that like for you?

- I had never been part of the decision making before. I just showed up and went to work. Now, it's like night and day, completely different. Now I can see the plan written down in an organized layout. We work in teams. We have goals. It's all been so shocking.
- You changed our church from a "they" church to a "we" church. We all participate. Things change; nothing stays the same.
- I have participated in all of the children's programs, and I don't have kids. We need to keep the children's programs coming!

In chapter 2, I described the vacation Bible school that some of the folks at Wollaston had run the summer before I came. No children attended, so the adults took the class themselves.

As a former community coalition coordinator, I had many skills in organizing successful community events. I started to use these skills and teach the congregation organizational tools right from the start. In the last five years, our programs have become well known throughout the wider community. Beginning with the Healthy Kids Vacation Camp and the Super Kids Saturday programs, we invited the community into our church. We geared the programs to children and got permission from the school administrators to send flyers home with children at several nearby elementary schools. We added an annual children's marionette show during the winter school vacation. Members organized monthly Friday Family Film Nights. That grew into year-round Family Fun Nights. These events are open to the wider community. Sometimes the program includes a movie. Other times the activity is games or crafts. They occasionally hire professional entertainment for the families who come. These free programs are geared towards the wider community, and members of our church see this as ministry of outreach—our church is meeting a need in the community by providing a place for families to gather and enjoy themselves. Many of the congregation's newer members have come into the church by way of the outreach of our members. We do charge for some of our programs, such as the Healthy Kids Vacation Camp and the marionettes show, and we receive some grants from local agencies to help keep the costs affordable for families.

Thirty children are enrolled in Sunday school and the nursery, and several older teenagers help in the nursery and run the PowerPoint projector for our Sunday morning worship service. As we began to build the Sunday school from the ground up, one of our directors introduced us to the Workshop Rotation Model, which, over the course of six or seven weeks, teaches Bible stories using different learning styles.[2] We have a dozen volunteer teachers who work in teams.

Different teams teach the lessons they are best suited to: for example, cooking with the children, doing crafts with them, or teaching the lessons from the Bible. We also adhere to "Safe Church Policies and Procedures" for our Sunday school that require two adults present in each classroom at all times.[3] Many volunteers from our congregation organize and run the children's programs. I continue to organize the Healthy Kids Vacation Camp and am pleased with all the help from outside our church that we receive from youth groups who volunteer through City Mission Society of Boston's Urban Outreach Project. We all grow through these opportunities to serve our community.

I have enjoyed watching different people initiate programs through the church. As a turnaround pastor, I got used to participating in the planning of so many events, and I helped to get many of the programs off the ground. But as the members take more and more responsibility for the future of the church, I am asked to do less and less. To be perfectly honest, at one point, I had to deal with my own feeling of being left out. But that is what happens when the people are empowered to do their own work on behalf of the church. Isn't that how they grow and develop their own leadership? That was the goal, right?

Connecting to Our Denomination, The United Church of Christ

After an estranged relationship with the Massachusetts Conference of the United Church of Christ, we have had many opportunities to welcome leaders from our conference here at Wollaston and to receive staff support in these past four years. What has it been like for you to ask for and to receive much-needed help and support from our denomination? Our church is becoming known in our community as a renewed and vital congregation, attracting new friends to our worshiping community. Not all people join, but we are called to provide hospitality to all. Can you give an example of how you have reached out to someone new?

- It's absolutely fantastic. There was never any communication from our former pastors about the conference or the United Church of Christ. It never even came up at a meeting. We wouldn't be receiving these grants today if we didn't have this relationship. It's very important.
- I feel as if our conference is embracing us as one of their children, and now they are coming to help us. They give us financial support, service by coming out to be with us. It's great to see they support you as a first time minister and they are not leaving you out there dangling all by yourself.
- We had no connection. It's good now.

The mission statement of the Massachusetts Conference of the United Church of Christ includes the phrase "nurturing local church vitality." To accomplish this, resources and staff support are available to the local churches through our state conference. Because Wollaston's connection with the conference had diminished over many years, they felt disconnected when I arrived. They simply did not know of the available resources. Although the Wollaston church had been one of the founding churches of the United Church of Christ when the denomination was formed in 1957, the folks who made that decision were long gone when I came in 2003. The congregation I met needed to be educated about its own roots in its denomination and to learn how to access conference resources. I knew about some of the resources and thought my responsibility was to build a bridge between our local church, our state conference, and our denomination's national staff and resources in Cleveland, Ohio. As we began to build relationships, we discovered the many resources available and how the denomination could help us in our situation.

Our congregation began to develop relationships with the denomination's state associate conference ministers, whom we invited to come to our church to worship with us, to eat with us, to preach to us, and to teach us. First came Carl McDonald, who was then the associate for Christian education. He gave us a lesson on hospitality and pointed out some of the challenges he, as a visitor, faced in coming to our church, For example, the building had no signs telling him where to enter. We hadn't provided childcare for our meeting, and that would prevent people with small children from attending the meeting. Tips like this helped us think about the small things we could to do to help families feel welcome in the church.

Andy Gustafson, the conference associate for stewardship, also offered support. Long before he helped us get started on our capital campaign, we invited Andy to preach before our congregation. During one Sunday morning worship service, Andy tied stewardship and faith together in his sermon by taking the emphasis off money and placing it on our financial giving as a matter of faith.

Paul Nickerson, our associate for evangelism and congregational vitality,[4] has become a familiar friend at Wollaston. Paul has been our vitality coach and has helped our congregation develop a heart for the mission field around Wollaston. He prepared for his visit with us by researching the current demographic information on Wollaston and on the neighborhood, which he shared with the congregation. This information was an education to us as we began to discover the neighborhood around the church and to see how Wollaston and the wider city of Quincy had changed so dramatically over the last fifty years. He urged us to study these statistics to get to know the church's neighbors and to pray about how our church could do ministry within our current context. He encouraged us to build on some of the community outreach programs we had developed. He urged us to pray that God would show us the needs of the current community and how our church could connect with those around us. He called this our mission field and helped us identify some of the needs close to home. Paul became the vitality coach for our congregation with frequent visits to our church and meetings with our members. Jim Griffith, a national church vitality consultant who specializes in coaching new church starts and turnaround churches,[5] often accompanies Paul on visits to Wollaston. Funded by our conference and Commission for Evangelism and Church Vitality, both Paul and Jim have helped our congregation discover the world right outside our doors, the neighborhood they call our mission field. From my perspective, they have constantly encouraged me to teach the members to look beyond the walls of the church to discover that the heart of our mission field is our neighborhood, which has taught us new ways to reach out to our local community. Both Jim and Paul often remind us to remember that although we are not yet a "full service church," in time we will grow into one. But for now, we should "act our size" and do the things we do very well. Clearly, God has a plan for us.

Our congregation has come to know these and others as champions of Christ who have worked tirelessly on behalf of all of the churches in our conference and have taken a special interest in our turnaround. Successful turnarounds are still rare throughout the mainline Protestant church, which makes telling the story of this success a crucial part of our church's ministry. We owe much credit to our conference leaders who have encouraged us along the way. Members of our church have developed strong ties to their denomination over these past six years, and these relationships have changed the way the congregation thinks and feels about the denomination. Members have come to know real people they can call on when in need. But even beyond the individual needs of Wollaston, the congregation has gained a real spiritual appreciation for how we and our individual church connect to our denomination and are a part of the wider body of Christ. What was once just a denominational name has become alive and a part of us. Being part of something much larger than our own congregation has encouraged some members to become active as representatives at our conference's annual meetings and to attend our area meetings. We are connected to a denomination that embraces those things that we hold most dearly. Those things include deep and abiding faith and practices as outlined in the United Church of Christ's Statement of Faith and the covenant among churches in Christ. Because of the generosity of many people in our conference, our church has been helped to discover its mission in Jesus Christ.

Worship, Stewardship, Leadership as Precursors to Mission

The members of the Wollaston church have learned that as an organization our church must adapt to constant change to meet the needs of people today in a rapid-paced, technologically advancing, and environmentally toxic society. To become a part of the heartbeat of the community, we had to get outside the church to reacquaint ourselves with the needs of our own neighbors. The congregation can no longer exist in a vacuum separated from the world outside its doors. All this change requires leaders who can convey a sense of optimism, enthusiasm, and creative confidence. Today's leaders must take risks and take the church to places the members never dreamed of going before. The church can no longer afford the luxury of marking time. Stagnation will lead to death. It is only a matter of time.

These are urgent times for pastors and congregations to understand that the world has changed and the ways in which we think and do church must also change. Today's pastors must be able to foster leadership in others who will mobilize the congregation into action. These actions for us at Wollaston included changing our worship service, education, and action in stewardship and developing leaders who can inspire action in others. This positive energy is infectious. Our congregation has learned to thrive in the midst of the chaos of constant change. We have overcome tremendous odds to create a future. The changes in worship, stewardship, and leadership that I have described in these last three chapters were the right formula for our church, but they may vary from church to church. These changes might seem to have taken a long time. But during this time, we have fallen more deeply into the heart of God's mission field right outside our doors. We believe that God has called us to be an example of hope to others. And in the next chapter, I will tell you about how we are spreading that hope around and how the tools of our congregation's turnaround have sparked inspiration for life-sustaining change.

Chapter 5

Vision and Mission

Jesus said, "Those who find their life will lose it, and those who lose their life for my sake will find it."
—Matthew 10:39

The options for the future of a dying church can be limited. One possibility is to once again become a growing and vital church. With that vision in sight, the mission is to do everything possible to make that happen, to resurrect the dying. In this situation, the underlying theme of both vision and mission is survival, while the driving question on everyone's mind is, "Can we make it?" This was true at Wollaston.

By *mission*, I mean the fundamental purpose of any organization, and by *vision* I mean a desired or intended future state of that organization. Organizational planners will agree that both mission and vision stem from shared beliefs and values. Although the members of the Wollaston church agreed on their faith beliefs and values, they did not all believe their church would survive. With only enough money to stay open for three more years, some thought the money would simply run out. Others believed in miracles and never stopped praying for new life for their church.

Wollaston was a dying church when I arrived. An interim pastor had served the congregation for a year and a half before I came in 2003. During his leadership, members of the search committee had written new vision and mission statements:

Vision Statement (2002)

The Vision of this Church shall be to commit ourselves, spiritually and materially, to spread the gospel and teachings of Christ. We will strive to make our church grow in every way.

Mission Statement (2003)

As a welcoming and caring church family, we dedicate ourselves in fellowship and God's Love in service to each other, the community, and the world. Empowered by the Holy Spirit, we are called and commit ourselves to worship God through music, prayer, and Christian love; to praise God, accept His forgiveness and joyfully proclaim the gospel; and to embrace and accept all people as Children of God with their own unique gifts.[1]

Although these statements were beautifully written, the members I talked with about the process remembered it with a collective groan. When survival of their church was at question, no number of pretty words was going to make it better. If a dying church is going to turn around and become vital in its community, the congregation has to begin with a frank discussion about its options and a more realistic view of what they need in order to have something to offer that community. I have written a lot about denial in this book, but I believe that writing these two statements was premature and not a matter of being in denial. Members of the congregation needed to consider how and if they were going to save their own church before they could even think about helping others. Initially, saving their church needed to be at the heart of both their vision and their mission.

In light of the situation, the members might have done better to agree on several attainable goals, to see if they could reach those before worrying about what their mission and vision were. They had immediate needs themselves and had to address what was going on inside their church before they could begin to reach out. In 2002 and 2003, their newly written vision and mission statements really didn't reflect their congregation or their own needs.

Mission Activity in 2003

Wollaston had a mission committee when I arrived. Money was collected and distributed among four local agencies. In addition, pennies were collected each fall and, with a special Thanksgiving food offering, were given to Interfaith Social Services of Quincy. The congregation would buy and distribute Christmas gifts for one or two community families. A few special collections were taken during the year to help support the denomination's mission outreach. So, some mission activity was going on in the church. Yet, in a city of more than one hundred thousand people, surely other needs were yet to be discovered. There was one member, in fact, whose heart was on fire to do missionary work somewhere. She wanted direction, and eventually that desire led her to spend three weeks in East Africa doing mission work. Perhaps her heart was burning to discover the potential within our congregation too, so that we could become a church with a wider mission to serve.

These 2003 mission programs continue, but have been multiplied tenfold today. Now, the congregation contributes to all five of the annual mission collections of the denomination, which has earned our church the denomination's "5 for 5" designation. Our entire congregation is engaged in some type of mission project, beginning with the Sunday school's offerings to Heifer International. We began the Matthew Ministry program in which church volunteers cook meals for the Quincy Crisis Center and engage in a prison book ministry and a children's outreach program. Our congregation acts as a host site for traveling youth groups who come to participate in all sorts of mission projects in and around Boston. These outreach programs are organized by Boston's City Mission Society, which is the oldest multiservice center in New England. In the current year's budget, the church designated a percentage of our annual pledges to mission outreach. These signs of giving of time, talent, and treasure are positive indicators that we are becoming more vital.

Paul Nickerson, our coach from the Massachusetts Conference of the United Church of Christ, has taught us that as we become more faith-filled people, our hearts are naturally turned towards giving and mission. He says first we must go inside ourselves to discover God's love within us, and then we move outward to share that love with others. Our conference's mission statement says the purpose of the Massachusetts Conference is "to nurture vitality in local churches and to strengthen the covenant among our churches." We have benefited from our conference staff and their living into this mission statement. Wollaston, as recipients of that nurturing, today would have a mission statement that includes radiating the vitality we have found within ourselves outward into our local community and beyond. The members I described as having an inward focus at the beginning of our journey together now look outward and are asking themselves, "Who's not here yet?" They are making it their mission to bring others inside to be opened to the transformative power of God's love that they have found and need to share. With each year that passes, members of the church have put more distance between that old dying congregation and the new and vital community of faith they are continuing to become.

Now, six years later, Wollaston has grown much healthier and livelier through the process of long-term and life-sustaining change. After significant and persistent changes in worship, stewardship, and leadership, perhaps the congregation is ready to consider writing new statements. Based on the growth and the health of our congregation, my hope is that new statements will recognize the ongoing need to grow and change. We continue to deepen our faith together and reach out in mission and ministry.

But just a year ago I felt that I was losing my way. Not only had the congregation and the church changed dramatically, but so had I. God had focused my heart on this church to help in its resurrection, but then I found myself back to my question: What was my call?

Then an injury to my Achilles tendon slowed me down enough so that I could reflect on my first five years as both a minister and a pastor of a turnaround church. I had time to spend with my spiritual director discerning where God was leading me next. During that time it was revealed to me that worship, stewardship, leadership, and mission had deeper layers yet to be discovered. I should stay on this course but lead the congregation to a deeper level. This notion was both uplifting and a little scary to me. When I was called to Wollaston in 2003, none of us had even heard the term *turnaround church*, much less known we would become one. None of us really knew the work that lay ahead of us. But now in 2009, we do know something about that work, and God has invited us back in for another round. I, along with the congregation, have accepted this new call to serve this new church within our old church. We came from the wilderness, and now we shall enter it again. Isaiah 40:3–5 reminds us that *it is in the wilderness* that we are to prepare a way for the Lord.

A voice cries out:

"In the wilderness prepare the way of the Lord,
make straight in the desert a highway for our God.
Every valley shall be lifted up,
and every mountain and hill be made low;
the uneven ground shall become level,
and the rough places a plain.
Then the glory of the Lord shall be revealed,
and all people shall see it together,
for the mouth of the Lord has spoken."

God's Transforming Work

In this book I have shared the story of the members of the Wollaston Congregational Church United Church of Christ in both my words and theirs. I hope that I have conveyed both the pain of loss and change as well as the possibility and hope of growth. It took drastic measures for the members of our church to be transformed from near death to new life. Becoming a welcoming church, embracing new members, welcoming children in worship, developing a Sunday school, recruiting teachers, renovating the Christian education wing of the building all engaged members in this process. Calling seminarians to bring new voices and shared leadership to the pulpit strengthened the church in its purpose. Worship music has changed dramatically, evolving over these past six years from the tentative whispers of a few to a ringing chorus of "Alleluia!" by everyone.

Individual financial commitments, reporting methods, and communications have all improved. Our capital campaign was successful. We continue to expand and develop our resources. Our building is now listed as historically significant in our state and nation, and we are looking for financial resources to make necessary repairs. New jobs have been created to expedite the many administrative tasks of operating the church.

We have developed new and effective ways to govern ourselves as a congregation, combining the voices of new and old members. New leaders continue to emerge with fresh ideas and energy to serve the church. Feedback from the community tells us that our outreach programs are excellent and are meeting needs in the wider community. Our members now feel connected to our denomination through the many relationships we initiated and continue to nurture with state and national denominational staff.

In Matthew 10:39, Jesus says, "Those who find their life will lose it, and those who lose their life for my sake will find it." Our members felt like they were losing their church. Yet, they were willing to take the many risks I have told you about, and do so in the name of Jesus Christ. And, as Jesus said, new life has been found for this church!

Now the church has let go of its old death grip and freely gives that new life away in so many ways. We are raising money to buy wells for villages in Africa, hosting monthly Family Fun Nights for the wider community, offering Healthy Kids Vacation Camps, preparing meals for the Quincy Crisis Center, engaging in and embracing the work of our wider denomination, and on and on.

The fruits of the turnaround at the Wollaston church are many, but perhaps none is greater than our witness to the transformative work of God's Holy Spirit in our midst. Through grace, we have been led to pass the church on to another generation of believers. For six years we have immersed ourselves in life-sustaining changes that will ensure the promise of a future for the church. The small group of people I met in 2003 has let go of and turned over the church life they knew, and in the process has given birth to a brand new church. Through telling you our story, we have become witnesses to the redemptive power of God's life-sustaining love. Now, what are you waiting for?

Notes

Chapter I

1. "Safe Church Policies and Procedures," Central Congregational Church (United Church of Christ), Chelmsford, MA, May 18, 2003, www.macucc.org/leadership/documents/ChelmsfordSafeChurchpolicies051903.pdf (accessed 2005).

2. This statement is part of "God is still speaking," also known as "The Stillspeaking Initiative," the name of the identity, branding, and advertising campaign of the United Church of Christ that was launched in 2004 (envisioned by Ron Buford, who served as the coordinator and spokesperson of the initiative until mid-2006).

3. Jan Karon, *At Home in Mitford* (New York: Penguin Books, 1999).

4. Caroline Myss, *Anatomy of the Spirit: The Seven Stages of Power and Healing* (New York: Three Rivers Press, 1996); Claudia Black, *Repeat After Me* (Denver: MAC, 1985); Hannah Hurnard, *Hinds Feet on High Places* (Wheaton, IL: Tyndale House, 1979); Sharon Wegscheider-Cruse, *Another Chance: Hope and Health for the Alcoholic Family* (Palo Alto, CA: Science and Behavior Books, 1989).

5. John Bradshaw, *The Family* (Deerfield Beach, FL: Health Communications, 1981); Rokelle Lerner, *Daily Affirmations for Adult Children of Alcoholics* (Deerfield Beach, FL: Health Communications, 1986).

Chapter 2

Thomas G. Long, *Beyond the Worship Wars: Building Vital and Faithful Worship* (Herndon, VA: Alban Institute, 2001), 15–20.

1. Myss, *Anatomy of the Spirit*.
2. Ronald A. Heifetz, *Leadership Without Easy Answers* (Boston: Harvard University Press, 1994).

Chapter 3

Scott Cormode, *Making Spiritual Sense: Christian Leaders as Spiritual Interpreters* (Nashville: Abingdon Press, 2006), xiii.

1. Sarah Drummond, Assistant Dean of Academic Affairs, Andover Newton Theological School. In 2004, Professor Drummond was my independent study director for my coursework on stewardship. In one of our meetings, she suggested I meet with Paul Adkins to learn about stewardship in his congregation. When I reported to Sarah what I learned from Paul, she gave me this phrase to make the information easier to remember and accessible to my situation at Wollaston. After one church member and I spent months cleaning out overstuffed closets in the church, we knew about getting our hands dirty.

2. George Barna, *Turn-around Churches: How to Overcome Barriers to Growth and Bring New Life to an Established Congregation* (Ventura, CA: Regal Books, 1993), 68–69.

3. The Wollaston Congregation Church United Church of Christ received funding to launch a pilot program called Pastoral Residency for Turnaround Ministry in the fall of 2009. Funds were also granted to develop a seminary course called "Turnaround Ministry." These funds were granted by the E. Rhodes and Leona B. Carpenter Foundation. For more in-

formation, visit www.wollycong.org or Rev. Dr. Mary Louise Gifford at wollcongchurch@comcast.net.

Chapter 4

Robert Smyth, "You're Welcome," *For My Brothers* (Cambridge, MA: Yellow Moon Press, 1978), 2.

1. Lyle E. Schaller, *A Mainline Turnaround: Strategies for Congregations and Denominations* (Nashville: Abingdon Press, 2005), 18.

2. Workshop Rotation Model, http://www.rotation.org/index.html (accessed 2005). The Workshop Rotation Model for Sunday school began in 1990 when a Presbyterian church in Chicago decided it was time to reinvent Sunday school or close down. In 1997 www.rotation.org was created to provide resources, lesson plans, and community conferences.

3. "Safe Church Policies and Procedures," Central Congregational Church (United Church of Christ), Chelmsford, MA, May 18, 2003, www.macucc.org/leadership/documents/ChelmsfordSafeChurchpolicies051903.pdf (accessed 2005).

4. Paul Nickerson, Associate Conference Minister of Evangelism and Church Vitality, Massachusetts Conference of the United Church of Christ (www.macucc.org/evangelism/index.htm).

5. Jim Griffith, Griffith Coaching Network (www.griffith-coaching.com).

Chapter 5

1. Vision Statement and Mission Statement, Wollaston Congregational Church, Quincy, MA, 2002–2003, www.Wollycong.org.